Global Citizenship Education for Young Children

Designed to assist educators of young children in building their awareness of their roles as members of a global community in an increasingly divided world, this essential guide is an illuminating resource which answers the question: "Is it possible to teach global citizenship in the first five years of life?" *Global Citizenship Education for Young Children* takes a close look at the practice of two preschools with vastly different histories, curricula and demographics and introduces readers to the range of possibilities that exist within early childhood global citizenship education. Snapshots of practice, strategies to employ and opportunities for self-reflection provide readers with concrete guidance for how to build learning environments that encourage global citizenship in the first years of life.

Robin Elizabeth Hancock, Ed.D., is an early educator, teacher trainer and global education specialist. Her practice is dedicated to supporting educators, both in the United States and abroad, who are working to build responsive global education experiences for their children and communities.

Other Eye On Education Books Available from Routledge
(www.routledge.com/k-12)

**Effective Family Engagement Policies: A Guide for
Early Childhood Administrators**
Teresa S. McKay

**Alphabetics for Emerging Learners: Building Strong Reading
Foundations in PreK**
Heidi Anne E. Mesmer

**Trauma-Responsive Family Engagement in Early Childhood:
Practices for Equity and Resilience**
Julie Nicholson and Julie Kurtz

**Relationship-Based Early Childhood Professional Development:
Leading and Learning for Equity**
Marilyn Chu and Kimberly Sopher-Dunn

The Kinderchat Guide to the Classroom
Heidi Echternacht and Amy Murray

**The A in STEAM: Lesson Plans and Activities for
Integrating Art, Ages 0–8**
Jerilou J. Moore and Kerry P. Holmes

Global Citizenship Education for Young Children

Practice in the Preschool Classroom

Robin Elizabeth Hancock

NEW YORK AND LONDON

Cover image: © iStock

First published 2023
by Routledge
605 Third Avenue, New York, NY 10158

and by Routledge
4 Park Square, Milton Park, Abingdon, Oxon, OX14 4RN

Routledge is an imprint of the Taylor & Francis Group, an informa business

© 2023 Robin Elizabeth Hancock

The right of Robin Elizabeth Hancock to be identified as author of this work
has been asserted in accordance with sections 77 and 78 of the Copyright,
Designs and Patents Act 1988.

All rights reserved. No part of this book may be reprinted or reproduced or utilised
in any form or by any electronic, mechanical, or other means, now known or
hereafter invented, including photocopying and recording, or in any information
storage or retrieval system, without permission in writing from the publishers.

Trademark notice: Product or corporate names may be trademarks or registered trademarks,
and are used only for identification and explanation without intent to infringe.

Library of Congress Cataloging-in-Publication Data
Names: Hancock, Robin Elizabeth, author.
Title: Global citizenship education for young children : practice in the
preschool classroom / Robin Elizabeth Hancock.
Description: New York, NY : Routledge, 2022. |
Series: Eye on education |
Includes bibliographical references.
Identifiers: LCCN 2022012204 (print) | LCCN 2022012205 (ebook) |
ISBN 9780367417253 (hardback) | ISBN 9780367437060 (paperback) |
ISBN 9781003005186 (ebook)
Subjects: LCSH: Education, Preschool–Social aspects. |
World citizenship–Study and teaching (Preschool) |
Culturally relevant pedagogy.
Classification: LCC LB1140.5.S6 H36 2022 (print) |
LCC LB1140.5.S6 (ebook) | DDC 372.21–dc23/eng/20220427
LC record available at https://lccn.loc.gov/2022012204
LC ebook record available at https://lccn.loc.gov/2022012205

ISBN: 978-0-367-41725-3 (hbk)
ISBN: 978-0-367-43706-0 (pbk)
ISBN: 978-1-003-00518-6 (ebk)

DOI: 10.4324/9781003005186

Typeset in Optima
by Newgen Publishing UK

Contents

Preface vii
Acknowledgments ix

Introduction 1

PART I: DEVELOPMENT, EARLY EDUCATION AND GLOBAL CITIZENSHIP EDUCATION 9

1. Early Childhood Development 11
2. Global Perspectives on Early Childhood Global Education 19
3. What is Global Citizenship? 36

PART II: GLOBAL CITIZENSHIP EDUCATION IN PRACTICE: LITTLE SUN PEOPLE 43

4. Little Sun People: The Context of Community 45
5. Little Sun People: Lessons in Power 59
6. Little Sun People: Self-Esteem Development 74

PART III: GLOBAL CITIZENSHIP EDUCATION IN PRACTICE: MID-PACIFIC INSTITUTE 93

7. Mid-Pacific Institute: The Context of Community 95

Contents

8. Mid-Pacific Institute: Membership in Community   111

9. Mid-Pacific Institute: Stewardship   128

PART IV: THE WORK OF TEACHERS   143

10. Self-Reflection   145

11. Collaboration   153

Afterword   162

Appendices   164

Preface

January 6, 2021.
It's mid-afternoon in month ten of a global pandemic. The Dean of Student Life and I have been hard at work (on a Zoom call from our respective homes) putting the finishing touches on a virtual fundraiser for a local organization tackling global food insecurity that our students have been committed to collaborating with for years. At 2:30 pm our phone alerts begin to ping at the same time. Every outlet is breaking the news simultaneously: the Capitol building in Washington, DC is under attack. For the next several hours we are glued to our devices as images and commentary inform us that thousands of people, enraged at the results of the recent democratically held election and armed with guns, bullet-proof vests, Nazi emblems, confederate flags, zip ties and at least one noose, have descended on the Capitol and forced their way inside. The image of a makeshift gallows rudely constructed outside the Capitol is stunning. The sound of the alternating chants of "USA, USA" and "Hang Mike Pence!" combined with the images of capital police like Black officer Eugene Goodman skillfully maneuvering the rabid crowd away from the politician's chambers is a surplus of violence and irony we are still attempting to untangle. Five people are killed. The echoes of anger and pain remain long after the Capitol has been cleared that evening.

January 10, 2019.
"You have been sold a lie… whether you like it or not, the world we live in is global. We can only fix this rigged system if we cooperate across borderlines."

~David Lammy, MP, British Labour Party. Brexit Speech. House of Commons.

November 2nd, 2014.

It's early in the morning at Little Sun People. A small child walks across the designated walkway to the Zulu Fouriors classroom where six children are sitting at two tables eating breakfast. A teacher at the entrance of the two year old room motions to Mama Aaliyah. "He's coming your way!" she says with raised eyebrows. Mama Aaliyah nods with a knowing smile. "Coming to see his friends." The toddler stands between the cubbies and the circle time rug, surveying the space. "Good morning, Kofi. How are you this morning?" A smile touches his face. He goes over to one of the tables and begins to pull at a chair bigger than he is. Makeda, a four year old at the table, stands up. "Kofi, you can't do that on your own", she says through a mouthful of egg and moves to assist him. "Let him do it." Makeda stands still and watches him skeptically, not yet sitting down. Kofi pushes and pulls the chair clumsily, until there is just enough room for him to squeeze his chubby body between the chair and the table and up onto the seat. Makeda laughs and wraps her arms around his neck, squeezing him until he begins to fuss. Mama Aaliyah brings him graham crackers and a cup of juice. "We missed you Kofi." "Yep", chimes Makeda, "Kofi has two classrooms, his and ours, right Mama Aaliyah?" Mama Aaliyah chuckles. "The whole school is his, right Kofi?" Kofi stays focused on his graham crackers, the crumbs gathering in his lap.

Reference

Lammy, D. (2019). *Brexit speech*. House of Commons, London.

Acknowledgments

This book would not be possible without the love and respect for children exhibited by the community of educators in my world. Special thanks to the administration and teachers at Little Sun People, Inc. and at Mid-Pacific Institute. Thank you to Fela Barclift, Aaliyah Barclift, Nikia Jenkins and Linda Clarke, and to Dr. Edna Hussey, Robynne Migita, Leslie Gleim and Jordan Hasley and all of their children. Many thanks to my former advisor at Teachers College, Dr. Celia Genishi, for her guidance these last twelve years. Thanks also to Marjorie Brickley, Judy Jablon, Ms. Cynthia Reed, Ms. Edna Elcock and the community of family child care providers in Brooklyn, New York, Dr. R L'Heureux Lewis-McCoy, Dr. Kadijah Matin, Yakeisha Scott and the educators of the International Reggio Exchange, for their generous contributions of expertise, resources, care and support. For the gift of seeking permissions, my gratitude to Tamieka Mosley and Anthony Leon. To my parents, Robert and Betty Hancock, thank you for everything.

Thank you to all of the children in all of the classrooms these last twenty years.

All of this is yours.

Introduction

The first semester of my doctoral program I was told that there was an ongoing conversation happening. My job as a scholar was to identify where I entered that conversation and with what to contribute. I've spent a considerable amount of time reflecting on what brought me to the conversation about global citizenship education and how who I am impacts what I teach and why. I enter the conversation as a heterosexual, cis-gendered, Black/African American woman from a lower middle class background who currently occupies a position of privilege as the director of Global Learning and Community Engagement at a prominent independent school in New York City. I also enter as an early educator by training. I grew up in a community that believed, among other things, that every person is guided by a certain pull and began working with young children during my summers at home from college. My first class of preschoolers are now twenty-three years old. It has been the greatest privilege to support the development of happy and curious young children in the company of other like-minded educators and communities.

I also enter this conversation as the only child of hard-working, committed and intensely protective parents, their very last chance at a child. As a young girl (see Figure I.1), good people and beautiful places filled my heavily curated life and I was often sheltered away from what they perceived to be the dangerous elements of the world.

I remember many early days of watching the world pass by from behind a gate I was not allowed to open. By the time I had reached adolescence, I learned to escape by way of artists who had the ability to transport me to other parts of the world with perspectives completely different

DOI: 10.4324/9781003005186-1

Introduction

Figure I.1 The author at four years old

from my own. Frida Kahlo, Chinua Achebe, Jane Austen, Antonín Dvořák and Miriam Makeba were my constant companions. Simultaneously, in my hunger to draw closer to my own community, I began to mine for and devour the works of elder Black American standard bearers. Alice Walker, Rita Dove and Maya Angelou filled my shelves. Jacob Lawrence and Tom Feelings showed me how my community saw me and I fell in love with my reflection. Sitting on the floor of my father's study, Duke Ellington's triumphant *Ellington at Newport* album, with its astonishing "Diminuendo and Crescendo in Blue", was my first taste of jazz. Still, I was an introverted child. Fearful of the world and painfully shy, other people's experiences became my connection to communities that I felt acutely detached from.

In public middle school a social studies teacher had a profound influence on my worldview and my self-image. A Black woman from Texas with no children of her own, Clydette Messiah (see Figure I.2) had the freedom to travel internationally every year with her students. Dr. Messiah was breezy and confident, a hard grader who laughed loudly and called home to check on her students often. In the spring of my eighth grade year I was given the opportunity to go with her abroad. I remember clearly the sunlight streaming through my window the morning of my departure and the sounds of my mother and aunts chatting nervously downstairs. It was the first time I was leaving the country and my family gathered at the bus

Introduction

Figure I.2 Dr. Clydette Messiah on one of many visits to Florence

depot to see us off. We waved furiously as the coach pulled out of the parking lot. I remember falling in love with the view of the northern Italian countryside through the clouds and the absence of fear as we descended.

Once in-country, I watched as my teacher effortlessly navigated us through the canals in Venice, haggling, laughing with and sometimes chastising the locals, depending on the situation, all in Italian. We took pictures on the lip of Mt. Vesuvius, ate gelato in Florence until we were sick and spent days on dusty country roads chatting with residents in small villages about local saints and daily routines.

The experience was life altering for me because although I knew Black folks intimately who thrived and moved with confidence and joy, and although I had been around people from different cultural backgrounds all my life as a result of very good public schools in our small, diverse New England city, I had never seen someone that I identified with operate so comfortably with other people who were so different from them, so far from home.

In those moments my worldview was cracked wide open. Without realizing it, I began the process of defining myself as someone with the freedom to move about in environments of my choosing and the ability to connect with others, no matter their difference from me. The experience created the first of many personal connections to the world, a budding understanding of my place in it, a level of self-esteem that had not previously existed, and a desire to have the same impact on other children that she had had on me.

This is where I enter.

Introduction

There is a subset of global education scholars who generally agree that global citizenship education has not yet been recognized as having a meaningful impact in early childhood spaces (Meyers, 2010). I was curious about why this was. As a researcher, preschool teacher and global educator, I have often been frustrated by the assumption that very young children do not have the capacity to develop an awareness of their positionality within the world around them. Any person intimately involved in the life of a young child will tell you that this is, of course, not true. Children begin an exploration of their surroundings at birth, and in their first five years rapidly develop the skills that they will use for the rest of their lives to analyze and make meaning of the world. The failure of research in the field of global citizenship education on its benefits to very young children as this process is happening is due, in part, to a lack of knowledge about these cognitive and socio-emotional functions. It is also due to disregard by the general public towards the capacity of early educators (teachers, families and community members), and the spaces that they occupy, to support the lessons that lead to the development of successful global citizens. This is an unfortunate oversight because among these lessons, empowerment, positive self-esteem development, membership in community and stewardship to the world around them are ones which are often naturally occurring in high-quality early education spaces.

Early in my teaching career, I was often disillusioned with traditional multicultural education (that particular experience of religions, holidays, food and song that takes up between five and fifteen days of the year, depending on how "progressive" the school is) because it was not sufficient to destabilize the racism, division and hypernationalism that is baked into the experience that children, regardless of race or socio-economic status, regularly encounter in schools and life (see Figure I.3) and which cause many of them profound social and emotional trauma. The culpable curriculum often reinforces an "us vs. them" mentality that inculcates young children early in life with the belief that some of them are more valued and meant to take up more space in the world than others.

As a result of this messaging, some of these young children grow into adults who believe that they are less worthy of their voices being heard, their needs being met and their multi-faceted identities being acknowledged. Others become adults who, having grown up unaccustomed to attention being placed anywhere other than on their own lived experience, respond with panic, violence and aggression towards their fellow human beings

4

Introduction

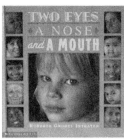

Figure I.3 The original cover of *Two, Eyes, a Nose and a Mouth* (which has since been revised in newer editions), the Cream of Wheat box featuring Chef Rastus, and the recently retired image of Chief Wahoo of the Cleveland Indians. These images, and others like them, serve as early visual indicators that inform children of their value, purpose and positionality in the world

whenever their position is perceivably threatened. I identify global citizenship education as a means of speaking back to this dangerous trajectory and removing the illusion of separateness that often begins early in a child's life.

With very few exceptions (the work of Homa Tavangar stands out in particular) the field is almost void of work that effectively articulates the value of global citizenship education in early childhood spaces. As such, there is little to guide early educators in search of global education teaching strategies that are both developmentally appropriate and culturally responsive. The discourse, where it does exist, has lived almost exclusively in the upper grades and, even there, subjects like social studies, world history, literature and economics are often taught in ways that consistently fail to educate about the value of and successes within Third World histories or to elevate them in the same ways that European contributions to the subjects are valorized (Ukpokodu, 2010). This means that wide swaths of young people spend their entire educational careers without being given an accurate understanding of what it means to live in a world with other individuals, cultures and communities that are just as complex, meaningful and valuable as their own.

This also means that early years teachers, as well as the families and communities that they serve, have been largely left out of the conversation about what it means to create and practice global citizenship education. This is troubling as the research shows that as early as two years

5

Introduction

old, children are using racial differences to reason about behavior (www. childrenscommunityschool.org) and at five years old (regardless of their race), have already been exposed to as many as 500 social indicators that inform them of their value and their "place" in their local and global communities (Hancock, 2015). These indicators, which will shape their understanding not only of their own worth but also their relationship to others, include everything from billboards on the side of the city bus to the images on their cereal box to their favorite cartoon character to the ways that their teachers respond to them in their first classrooms. This book addresses the intersection of early childhood education and global citizenship education. Here, two early learning centers, similar in some ways and profoundly different in others, speak for themselves about what it looks like to educate preschool-aged children to be members of a global community and why this kind of education is so important at an early age.

So what exactly is early childhood global citizenship education and what does it look like in practice? To answer those questions, it's helpful first to ground ourselves in a snapshot of how young children's brains develop from birth to the fifth year of life and how they come to understand who they are in relation to the world around them during this time. It is also useful for us to locate the practice of global citizenship education in the United States within the constellation of philosophies that have guided educators around the world in their practice of early childhood global education. Doing so will help us position early childhood global citizenship education as a useful pedagogy within the ongoing conversation about what "good" early childhood education is.

References

Children's Community School. www.childrencommunityschool.org

Hancock, R. (2015). *All of this is yours: Global citizenship education as emancipatory practice for African American preschoolers*. Teachers College, Columbia University.

Meyers, J. (2010). 'To benefit the word by whatever means possible': Adolescents' constructed meanings for global citizenship. *British Educational Research Journal, 36*(3), 483–502.

Tavangar, H. (2009). *Growing up global: Raising children to be at home in the world*. Ballantine Books.

Ukpokodu, O. (2010). Teacher preparation for global perspectives pedagogy. In B. Subedi (Ed.), *Critical global perspectives: Rethinking knowledge about global societies* (pp. 121–142). Information Age Publishing, Inc.

PART

I

Development, Early Education and Global Citizenship Education

1 | Early Childhood Development

The ways that children make sense of the world and their positionality in it begin much earlier than many people believe. Thousands of books have been written about early childhood development. For the sake of this text, this chapter focuses on the particular elements of development that contribute to young children's developing sense of themselves in relation to others. What happens in these early months and years is valuable context to the conversation about the possibilities within early childhood global citizenship education because it provides us with insight into how the young child begins not only to see the world but how they fit into and learn to impact that world in the first years of life.

At birth babies are hardwired to engage with the world as quickly as they can for survival's sake. A newborn's rooting, twisting and crying are some of the things that many humans have been genetically trained to find irresistible and the arms of a sheltering adult, motivated to respond to these indicators, is where the newborn finds their first safe place earth-side. Very soon after this, infants begin to be influenced by and develop preferences within their cultural space and will start to recognize the smells, sounds and tastes of this place that they will come to identify as home (Derman-Sparks, 2012).

As early as four months old, babies gaze at recognizable faces and study unfamiliar ones. They will need time to grow accustomed to the new sounds, smells and visual images that a new person brings and will voice their displeasure quickly if they do not want to make the shift to new arms or if they need more time for the shift to happen. At seven months, babies will express curiosity towards other babies. It can be an enjoyable

DOI: 10.4324/9781003005186-3

past-time observing what sometimes appears to be mutual recognition between infants who notice each other in public spaces. What seems like adoration of others who look like them is more accurately an early form of categorization that allows very young children to differentiate between other babies and adults. By their first birthday, most babies have become very good at this categorization. The urge to reach out and touch another baby within arms distance is an outward expression of this curiosity.

By fourteen months, "[young children] are starting to explore social skills, communicating without words, joining and not joining a friend [and] by eighteen months, a child will imitate much of the world around them" (Brazelton & Sparrow, 2006, p. 342). Our little one is a natural scientist, trying out and testing each new material and learning about their power to manipulate it. Making the leap from interpreting their surroundings as something separate from them to understanding the world around them as something that they have an impact on is a massive cognitive achievement. As a result, by eighteen months toddlers have begun to devote a great deal of time and effort to their symbolic play, for instance, building a tower as tall as themselves (see Figure 1.1) and then finding infinite joy in their ability to knock it down. The awareness that they are in control of both the tower's building and destruction becomes just as exciting as the mild sensory shock of the sound and sight of the blocks tumbling to the ground.

Figure 1.1 The discovery that the child has a direct impact on their surroundings is an extraordinary moment of self-discovery

Early Childhood Development

These experiences of the impact they have on their world will continue to be explored throughout their childhood and will help to teach them about their positionality in that world as they grow older. The ability to consider their environment, to change it, and the response their environment has to them as they engage in this exploration – responses of acceptance, encouragement, ambivalence or rejection – will inform them of their value, their ability and their sense of freedom and safety in the world, even now.

By eighteen months the young child has also learned to recognize themself in the mirror. They may spend an extended period of time examining their reflection, gazing at themselves, and pointing at their own features. It is a wonderful time of exploration and realization and a time when they will begin to be curious about the ways their bodies work. Simultaneously, it is a time when they will have already started to make sense of messages that they come in contact with about the value of their physical features.

As mentioned, our brains have developed over time to make sense of the world by sorting what we encounter into categories and the toddler brain is working overtime to do this work for them. These messages will come more and more rapidly as they are introduced to indicators in their world such as books, television, the conversations around them, their physical surroundings, etc., which will assign different values to themselves and others. The Children's Community School (2018) references Hirschfeld, who documented children as young as two years old connecting race to behavior and drew a direct link to their exposure to these social indicators. Sometimes adults worry that if they engage their children in an exploration of differences, it will encourage children to see things that they might not otherwise notice and lead them to discriminate. However, the science is clear that developmental sorting happens naturally (and early), whether we as adults engage children or not.

Often, the span between eighteen months and two years old is seen as an opportune time to begin to expose young children to interactions with their peers for longer periods of time. Firmly entrenched in this world of meaning-making, it is a great moment to give children opportunities to explore and articulate what it feels like to be in relationship with others. Alicia Lieberman (2018) identifies that it is here where we begin to see an "emerging ability to think about oneself and to make inferences about other people's point of view [which] has been called 'theory of mind' because it enables the child to make predictions about how other people think, feel and will behave" (p. 47). The two-year-old child who lives in a community

13

surrounded by people who accept her, love her and want her there will understand that she is accepted, loved and wanted and, as she grows, will move in ever-widening circles in the world with the understanding that acceptance and love towards her are reasonable expectations.

At three, with increased exposure to their peers and opportunities for play, children's experience with others is building a sense of confidence. Simultaneously, we see at this stage an increase in the development of empathy. When a child offers a toy, shares a piece of food with a friend, sits close to a playmate who is crying with notable concern or hands back a material dropped by an adult with joy, what we are witnessing is a more concrete understanding in the child that something is happening within someone else. Brazelton and Sparrow (2001) confirm this when they observe that with empathy "...[the child] can begin to understand that his world encompasses the needs and feelings of others, not just his own" (p. 38). Scaffolded learning is also occurring because the child understands, by now, that they can have an impact on these recognized feelings through their actions (see Figure 1.2) in the same way that they had an impact on their building blocks.

They are still very much in need of support in these explorations and safe, secure attachments with trusted adults provide a strong foundation on which to continue with confidence. A child with adults in their life

Figure 1.2 Expressions of care indicate that children are aware that others have feelings and needs as well

Early Childhood Development

who offer a secure base has the confidence to explore and the knowledge that they can come back to that base to be cared for and protected whenever they are in need (Bowlby, 1980). Armed with this support, young children enter an endless loop of 1) exploring with confidence and 2) seeking shelter in the safety and security of their community.

Lieberman (2018) notes that this learning about the world is the primary motivation of our busy three year old. Everything is something new and exciting and the majority of the child's time is spent making sense of it all. The human brain continues to problem solve rapidly. Leiberman states that "childhood is an early laboratory for the challenges and dilemmas of adult life... this period brings us face-to-face with two powerful impulses: the longing to feel safe in the protective sphere of intimate relationships and the exhilarating thrust of carefree, unrestricted, uninhibited exploration" (p. 13).

This desire for uninhibited exploration is joined, in the third year, by a form of pretend play that is used with greater fluency to build "their capacity to put themselves into the position of another person, when they understand that what they see from their specific physical location is not necessarily what other people see from their own different location" (Brazelton & Sparrow, 2001, p. 48). More complex than the realization that others feel things too, here the child is realizing, for the first time, that others don't necessarily think, feel or experience the world in the same way that they do. At this stage, children may observe or be very curious about such differences. They may ask lots of questions or be deeply reflective. The beauty here is that, although developmentally, our three- to four year old may not grasp the concept of the "global", what they are deeply engaged in is the experience of being a child and, by this time, can recognize both that other children exist and that those children may not necessarily have the same experiences or feelings as them.

Approaching four years old (Figure 1.3), the child is becoming concretely aware of the differences between themselves and other peers (as well as adults) and they will have already begun to vocalize their observations. "Why?" may be the question we hear the most from our inquisitive explorer and noticings will fill their conversations. It is a glorious time to engage children in an exploration of similarities and differences. They may want to touch a new person's face, hair and clothing but now, in addition, they "may feel [their] own hair and face to be sure of [their] own assets" (Brazelton & Sparrow, 2001, p. 347). What are perceived as socially

Figure 1.3 It is natural for children to ask questions about differences. The responses from adults help to inform them whether to be fearful or inclusive of those differences

controversial differences such as race, gender and ability will spark open and honest curiosity.

Again, the adult's role is one of safety and security, a place where the child can ask questions without judgment and receive answers without embarrassment or shame. In their effort to categorize and make sense of these differences, children are studying the adults in their lives and their reactions to new experiences. While fear is a natural response to the unknown, distaste, disdain and other negative emotions will come if the child observes, and then internalizes, the emotionally loaded responses of the adult during these explorations of differences. As the adults in young children's lives, it is not the observation of difference that we should attempt to suspend (it wouldn't work if we tried). Our work is in removing judgment from these conversations.

There are times when the inundation all around children of imagery loaded with judgment about which characteristics are valued and which are not can take the adult's place and has been shown to have a profoundly negative impact on the self-image of the young child. Psychologists Kenneth and Mamie Clarke's doll studies (1950) exposed the damage that these cultural indicators have. The research, which focused on African American children between the ages of three and seven, revealed that the derogatory images, beliefs and structures that children encounter at an early age were directly responsible for internalized beliefs about their own inferiority. We are now aware that when young children are surrounded by positive images and perceptions of themselves, they are more likely to develop into confident, emotionally healthy individuals.

Quite a lovely complement to the emotionally healthy child's awareness of the differences of others is a seemingly limitless capacity for connection and the development of friendships despite these differences. On my commute home, I pass by a large playground created to accommodate various developmental stages. The sun is usually setting and families are beginning to leave the playground and head home to their evening rituals. Inevitably, there is a child who is positively inconsolable at the thought of leaving their friend(s) behind for the evening. Usually an adult is present and attempting to explain that they will come back "later". While time can still be a complex concept for the average four- to five year old, the strong feelings that sometimes arise from being separated from their peers can be transparent and plain as day. As we'll see, the friendships children make at this age can be used as an organic and child-driven catalyst for explorations of authentic relationship building in the community with those who are both similar to and unlike them.

Knowing that children are exposed to indicators that inform them of their place and value in relation to others, the questions that children raise about difference at this age are wonderful opportunities to engage them in conversation about what they notice and to inquire into what about other people, different as they may be, make them beautiful, loved and/or important. The question becomes, how do we do this work effectively to support young children to become both healthy and confident in their own identities and good community members in the world? Globally, there are many theories about how to achieve this. It's worth exploring some of them to put the practice of global citizenship education in the United States in context.

References

Brazelton, T., & Sparrow, J. (2001). *Touchpoints three to six: Your child's emotional and behavioral development.* Perseus Books Group.

Brazelton, T., & Sparrow, J. (2006). *Touchpoints birth to three: Your child's emotional and behavioral development.* Perseus Books Group.

Bowlby, J. (1980). *Attachment and loss, vol. 1: Attachment.* Basic Books.

Children's Community School. (2018). www.childrenscommunityschool.org

Clarke, K. B., & Clarke, M. P. (1950). Emotional factors in racial identification and preference among negro children. *The Journal of Negro Education, 19*(3), 341–350.

Derman-Sparks, L. (2012). *Stages in children's development of racial/cultural identity and attitudes.* Sophia Lyons Fahs Lecture, UUA General Assembly.

Lieberman, A. (2018). *The emotional life of the toddler.* Simon & Schuster.

Global Perspectives on Early Childhood Global Education

It is within the extraordinary context of rapid early socio-emotional and cognitive brain development that global education can be most meaningful. It is also during this time, globally, when families are coordinating care for their youngest children and identifying the cultural lessons that are most important for children to experience at their early age. Some prioritize socialization in the community, while others are most concerned with preparing their children academically for a competitive world. Still others desire for their children to be exposed to perspectives outside of their experience at home. Some aspire to western ideals of early childhood education, taking pages from Montessori, Dewey and Ladson-Billings. Others reject this and lean into ideologies unique to their own communities.

The idea of what it means to educate young children well across the world has developed a bit like a rapidly flowing stream of water with tributaries of thinking flowing to it from all sides. The goal here is not to provide a comprehensive review of international theories regarding early childhood education. Rather, the purpose is to reflect on various philosophies around the world that are relevant to and inform the conversation about what global citizenship education in early childhood spaces can look like. In particular, it is interesting to see the type of global education which relies on the impact of the community and the environment on the life of the child and how it is enacted in different parts of the world. These snapshots of history and practice can help us understand the vast possibilities that exist in the practice of global citizenship education for very young children.

DOI: 10.4324/9781003005186-4

Japan

1872 is widely understood to be the beginning of the modern era of education in Japan (Duke, 2009) and is known as the era of Gakusei, or the "Education plan". Gakusei was influenced by the spread of western power's colonialism, which posed a threat to Japan's identity as a sovereign state. Three philosophies about education that reflect this tension existed at the time: Kangaku, which was based on Chinese culture and ways of learning; Wagaku, which was more oriented towards indigenous Japanese culture; and Yogaku, which represented all things western and was heavily influenced by the west's encroachment on Japanese culture. The government of 1873 set the goal of providing an education for every child in the country, regardless of their family's socio-economic standing. The result was a fusion of Japanese cultural tradition and western ideals.

For early education, children between the ages of six and fourteen were eligible to attend school and parents were obligated to enroll their children in the first four years. Instead of a curriculum that focused on morals, many textbooks and curricula in the Wagaku tradition were focused on admiration of the state. While developmentally appropriate themes such as play and cultural tales were present in the life of early educational spaces, teachers were encouraged to cover the span of Japanese history with a primary theme of love for country.

China

In China, the writings of celebrated educator Tao Xingzhi provide insight into the aspirations of Chinese early childhood education. Writing in the early first half of the 20th century, Xingzhi was inspired by his experience at Teachers College in New York City and with the giants in the field at the time such as Dewey but more so by his return to China and his desire to elevate the cultural values of his homeland. He believed in liberating the child by addressing each aspect of their life (Xingzhi, 2016). Upon his return after several years in the United States, Xingzhi worked to infuse the belief that early education should provide practical knowledge such as how to build and repair alongside more academic subjects.

Scholars of the time also believed that early education should make room for children's voice and questions. Effort was made to give children the opportunity to experience a sense of freedom to explore and be at home in nature. Attached to this was a valuing of and responsibility towards maintaining the natural world. Educators were encouraged to build moments into the life of the young child to explore this relationship.

Generally speaking, the goal of early education, according to Xingzhi, was to create "a world of happiness" (Xingzhi, 2016, p. 31) not for children but alongside and in partnership with them. This priority is seen in many parts of the world today, including in the Reggio Emilia philosophy to be explored later in the text. Through several iterations, the remnants of these values can be seen in modern Chinese early childhood education today.

India

For communities with young children in India, the common belief surrounding the birth of a child is that they are a gift from God (Swaminathan, 1998). In more traditional upbringings, parents possess a general confidence in their child's ability to navigate their world although many different caretakers and teachers occupy the young child's life before the age of six. Education has historically been divided between low and high caste with less privileged children often building knowledge informally through family-initiated instruction. Early documentation of education practices noted the grouping of children under the direction of a local guru; however, institutional learning was only available for the wealthy. An exception were Madrasas where neighborhood groups of boys could begin their education between five and six years old and where Quranic teaching and philosophy were primarily taught.

Prior to British colonial rule, the practice of education within Muslim communities in India was based on three principles:

- Knowledge as a religious obligation of all who practice Islam.
- Education that was free and unrestricted.
- Community members who were obligated to participate in providing it (Qureshi, 1975).

In this way, the poorest of families were assured the opportunity to educate their young children. From an early age, respect for the practice of education and discipline in its pursuit were messaged to children and teachers were deeply respected members of the community. Culturally, education was understood to be the means by which individuals could rise through the ranks to be successful and contributing members of society. With the introduction of British colonialism, however, Indians were no longer eligible for higher posts, no matter how advanced their education.

The attempted Rebellion of 1857 inspired many across the country to strengthen their community ties with fellow Muslims and paved the way for the eventual establishment of Pakistan. Included in this swell of pride was the creation of a number of schools for Muslim children. Thus, in Muslim communities, early education's primary aims became both to prepare youth to be employable and to reinforce a sense of community for a Muslim population in the midst of social and cultural change.

The arrival of the British also introduced a decidedly Christian orientation to schooling along with reading and writing. Although the British presence remained strong until their withdrawal from the country in 1947 (and after), indigenous systems of early education were continued by a large portion of the population which had had little contact with the British formal system. The non-violent movement for independence introduced the concept of Basic Education, inspired by Ghandi, which taught that all were equal, manual skills were highly valuable and emphasis on learning by doing for the youngest learners was reinforced. This was a direct response to the foreign British power's destabilizing influence on traditional Indian wisdom and philosophy and was a decided rejection of colonial values.

Saudi Arabia

The region of Saudi Arabia, governed mainly by Ottomans at the time, established a system of state schools exclusively for boys in 1880 (AlMunajjed, 1997). Formal education for girls was largely unavailable and most young girls, if educated, were taught at home. Despite this, literacy remained high, regardless of gender, until the discovery of oil in the 1930s. Two decades later, a ministry of education was established in 1953 and the first public schools were opened that year.

As more Saudi young adults began to travel abroad, the call was raised to formally educate young girls as well (the argument being that young men needed women educated at their level to ensure successful marriages).

In 1960, public education for girls began, backed by the rationale that educating young girls, at least in their Quranic studies, would prepare them to be better Muslim mothers. Thus the function of education became the means to strengthen the religious as well as the cultural values of the country, from one generation to the next.

Early education in Saudi Arabia begins at four years old. From their earliest classrooms, children are instructed based on gender-based cultural expectations with girls encouraged to learn sewing, cooking and home management along with their religious studies, Arabic and early math. In 2005, King Abdullah announced a major overhaul of the education system, in part to make it less resistant to non-Muslim perspectives. Change has been slow however as conservative clerics, whose perspectives helped found the country in 1923, wield a strong influence over educational materials used in the classroom.

 ## Egypt

In Egypt, learning was a form of worship. Madrasas were the site of most learning as early as 1097 with Saladin establishing the first Madrasa in Cairo in 1170 (Berkey, 1992). Families worked to connect their children with noted scholars and it was widely accepted that a student's success was often a result of their teacher's reputation just as much as their actual acquisition of knowledge. Early education focused on teaching the youngest children in the community to read and write. Literacy, even in the early years, is an expectation in the country today for this reason.

Education has also historically been a vehicle for cultural assimilation in the country. Slaves who were brought to Egypt from other parts of Europe and Asia at a very young age were converted to Islam, educated and assimilated into the culture through their education and utilized in the army to defend the vast lands held by the Islamic community. After a period of service, they were freed and often times entered public service, married and remained in the country.

A young boy's first educational task, after learning his letters, would be to commit the whole of the Quran to memory. Although pockets of society disapproved of girls being educated, there were communities of girls who were educated as well and several schools were either founded or endowed by women of the elite class as public acts of religious charity. The majority of families who sought to educate their young girls often utilized informal settings such as private homes. Communities with higher levels of education were especially keen to educate their daughters with women often educating younger children, a tradition that continues.

Ghana

Prior to independence in 1957, early childhood school curricula in Ghana were influenced heavily by missionaries and the British government (Ensor, 2012) and ran counter to the intent of Ghanaian independence, which was decolonization, self-actualization and Pan-Africanism. Kwame Nkrumah, the nation's first president, was himself a vocal Pan-Africanist who believed in the consolidation of power on the continent of Africa while resisting both political and economic influence from outside forces as a means of empowerment for Ghanaian citizens and, ultimately, all members of the African diaspora. Under Nkrumah, cultural activists advocated for children to experience recognizable elements of their culture in their school life.

Over time, conflict between traditional cultural practitioners and followers of the version of Christianity brought by the British developed. Elements of this tension remain today and it is sometimes seen as a contradiction to be both pro-culture and pro-Christianity. Regardless of this tension, children are highly valued in the community and are traditionally seen as representative of the nation's potential and future. Socialization of the child is considered to be the responsibility of their community (Ensor, 2012) and traditions that rely on and strengthen the community, such as Outdoorings when a newborn is officially introduced to their extended family and given their day name, begin early in the child's life.

Modernization has led more families to travel greater distances for work and, in some cases, to a breakdown of the traditional extended family structure, which has increased the need for formalized out of home early childhood care. While extended family are still utilized in the care of young children where possible, center based staff often see themselves as extensions of the family unit. Regardless of who is providing care, efforts to create early childhood curricula that reflect the life of the child are generally understood to be most effective (Mfum-Mensah, 2017). For instance, in northern Ghana, early lessons in literacy and numeracy that utilize contexts from young children's daily life (babysitting younger siblings, going to market, helping out on the farm, etc.) are seen as most effective by teachers at increasing both knowledge and confidence because they include content that children are most familiar with in other aspects of their lives.

Uganda

Although it is currently the second youngest nation (78% of people are under 30), indigenous knowledge is heavily influential in childrearing in Uganda. It is generally accepted that a number of voices, including that of the mother, are necessary for the successful rearing and education of the child (Kamusiime, 2019). Similar to many of the other communities named in this section, care of mother and child is traditionally distributed across the community with grandparents, older siblings and unrelated community members providing health, nutritional and financial support to the young mother.

Early care and education at home is the primary option for a majority of young children in the country. A child's first lessons include "dancing" them, which typically means nurturing their socio-emotional growth, fine and gross motor skills through interactive games, singing, dancing, counting, playing and holding them often. Gentle pet names such as *kamaama* (little mama) and *kyebeeyi* (treasure) accompany this play and reinforce bonding and a cultural acceptance of affection. Mothers are encouraged to motivate their children, particularly from developmental stage to stage, with excitement and mirroring alongside them which, along with extended family support, messages to the child that they exist within a community ecosystem of care.

South Africa

The oppressive system of apartheid in South Africa was designed to disempower its majority Black population and privilege White South Africans; the predominantly Dutch Afrikaner community as well as the English, both settler colonial communities who made South Africa their home due to its rich resources and strategic global positioning. Apartheid impacted all levels of education from (at least) 1948 until the early 1990s and remained official law until the democratic elections of 1994. H.F. Verwoerd, Minister of Native Affairs, was not subtle in 1953 when he declared his intention to teach Black children early that they did not have the right to equality with Whites in South Africa (Bloche & Prinsloo, 1998).

In response, a roiling, largely student-led resistance applied pressure against the overtly racist system and, in particular, the explicit ways that it impacted their education, across the country. A case in point: in 1980, the Committee of 81, made up of Black, Coloured and Indian students in the Western Cape, stated their refusal to back down from government pressure by stating that they would no longer be subject to the apartheid system and that the only acceptable future was one without racism and inequality. In the 1980s, adjustments were made to nation-wide early childhood education curricula but these were mostly in favor of White children's educational experiences and, to a lesser extent, Asian and Coloured or mixed race children. The impact of this is that Black children were consistently designated as unprepared for ongoing schooling.

After the elections of 1994, a promise was made by the African National Congress of one year of preschool alongside the promotion of the philosophy that school readiness meant that schools should be ready for children rather than that children be ready for school. It has been noted that previous constructions of education in South Africa, as it relates to Black children specifically, has addressed children's learning from a deficit-based lens. Efforts have been made to shift this and it is more accepted today that the child's education be approached from a holistic perspective. For instance, it is generally accepted now that early literacy can be learned in school from book reading as well as at home through indigenous and generational traditions of oral storytelling, etc.

Greece

When we turn to Europe, both historical and contemporary models draw attention to how early education situates young children in the local and global community. In ancient Greece, with both high birth and mortality rates during the Early Iron Age (1000–700 BCE) it's likely that upwards of 40% of the population was under the age of eighteen. Langdon (2013) suggests that it would benefit a society with this number of young people to invest resources in their well-being, in particular their socialization into functioning members of society; for example, a society organized where children begin to learn skills such as textiles and pottery under the tutelage of an adult or senior adolescent early in life. The presence of miniature vessels found in archeological digs doesn't simply imply small hands created them but that cognitive and fine motor skills as well as cultural mastery (including the involvement of the very young in religious ceremony) were priorities in the life of the ancient Greeks. Looking at the lumpy, awkward productions one can imagine furrowed brows and small, chubby hands manipulating clay in much the same way that children in today's classroom might attack the curious and inviting material.

Early childhood ritual served as a means of community cohesion. On the baby's fifth day it was presented to the family, marking its entry into the community. On the seventh day, relatives and friends traditionally brought gifts, marking the day the baby was officially introduced to the wider family. Most often, as part of the welcoming ritual, parents would dress their infant with protective amulets and invoke the protection of a set of deities. In addition, rites of passage provided young children with an education in the relationship between humans and gods as well as practice in independence, bravery and critical thinking; all skills which would benefit them as adults. For instance, the practice of "Choes" or "Pitchers", which typically occurred in the child's third year, was an event where they were introduced to their peer group and where, it has been speculated, the child was exposed to an environment for the first time where adults other than their mother provided guardianship. There is also evidence that young children took part in religious ceremony as bakers, officiates, intermediaries and as members of choruses.

Finland

Globally, Finnish early education has been hailed as one of the most successful in achieving high-quality standards (Aslan, 2020). Historically, Finland has also existed in a politically crucial location between east and west. As a result, political and religious tensions exist due to previous Swedish and Russian rule. Catholic and Protestant influence still permeate the country although both independence in 1917 and the Freedom of Religion Act in 1923 have meant that no priority or preference can be given to any one religion.

A side effect of these changing identities was the 2016 update to the National Core Curriculum for Early Childhood Education and Care, which now provides mandatory instruction in worldview education. The instruction allows children to develop an awareness of other identities as well as the opportunity to practice ways that are sustainable and beneficial to the global community. Seen by educators and administrators as ethically responsible to implement early in a child's life, the curriculum is taught through increased exposure to a diversity of perspectives. In classrooms, young children benefit from the gradual learning of different traditions but also through regular interaction with community members whose worldviews differ from their own.

France

France provides the curious case of a network of summer camps that were created through various charities for working class families in France and the influence it had, and continues to have, on the idea of early education within the country. The first recorded example of a *colonie* in Europe was initiated by Wilhelm Bion, a pastor in Sweden who took it upon himself to take a large group of children from Zurich's poorest communities on holiday to the mountains. Inspired by this and by social concerns over the growing health issues young low-income children faced in France's crowded and dirty streets at the turn of the century, Edmond Cottinet, a wealthy philanthropist, developed a similar model, the *colonies scolaires*. From this grew the *colonies de vacances*, which spread throughout the country.

Beginning in the early 1900s, thousands of children from low-income communities left their families in the warmer months and traveled to the countryside or near the coast for "camp" (Downs, 2002). In this way, the *colonies de vacances* became a common experience for most working class children. Many (although not all) citizens who attended as children have reflected positively on their experiences spent in the fresh air of the countryside. Studies of the nation-wide retreats also forced a larger conversation on the quality of early childhood development and education, which was documented as being noticeably improved by children's experiences in these natural surroundings, which has led to reforms.

Colombia

In South America, early education philosophy varies from country to country and in many places honors indigenous knowledge as paramount. Other countries look to the global north (namely the United States) as their standard for high-quality education. Colombia has made significant progress in the last several years in the fields of education, development and health and nutrition. De Cero a Siempre is a program implemented by the state department to address children's rights and has created a strategy which engages numerous agencies across the country in the task (Schwartzman, 2015). A key element of the strategy is to locate children from birth to six years old, as well as pregnant mothers and their immediate families, at the center of communities in order to focus on their support and development.

Embedded in this structure of support is the understanding that each child is different (developmentally, emotionally, culturally, etc.) and their care and education ought to reflect this reality. It also recognizes that children cannot be effectively cared for or educated separate from their family and community. This challenges several other philosophies, including that of Catholicism's colonial education legacy, present in several other Latin American countries as well, which stressed the separation of the child from their family, community and "cultural ways of knowing" to achieve its aims in residential schools.

Jamaica

During slavery, young children in Jamaica were often cared for by the elderly or sick while their families worked long hours on plantations or in the plantation's big houses (Daley & Thompson, 2004). For a time after Emancipation in 1834, the Methodist, Baptist and Presbyterian churches present on the island ran a series of "Infant Schools", which provided basic education to a wide age range of children. Over the years, many non-profit organizations supported various parishes' educational efforts. The Project for Early Childhood Education (PECE) was a partnership created between the government of Jamaica and the Bernard van Leer Foundation. Early learnings found that parent–teacher relationships were key to the healthy development and successful education of young children. A primary goal was to educate children to be competitive performers once they reached higher education. The program, based at the University of the West Indies, trained teachers in a triangular relationship between themselves, their children and their children's families which reflected the values of collaboration that already existed in various forms in the community.

Much like their African and South American counterparts, Jamaican educational scholars such as Roopnarine and Brown (1997) identify healthy family environments as the primary tool for early childhood socialization. Inspired by the United Nations Sustainable Development Goals, there is an understanding among policy makers and educators that "whole child" care is a community effort. Along with healthy families, quality programming that effectively integrates health, education, safety and community in Jamaica is a necessity for very young children to grow into curious, joyful and action-oriented citizens.

Canada

Education in colonized spaces has often been used in the attempt to disempower indigenous communities. One such community in Canada are the Dene, members of the Northern Athabaskan Council. For the Dene, education has always been an aboriginal and human right formalized in multiple treaties (Abu-Saad & Champagne, 2006). Prior to the arrival of missionaries, the Dene had a complex and responsive system of education that reinforced a strong sense of community, identity and widely held beliefs about their relationship with the land. "She is a teacher, a teacher who punishes swiftly when we err, yet a benefactress who blesses abundantly when we live with integrity, respect her, and love the life she gives" (Lamothe, 1977, pp. 10–11). We now know that many missionary schools, a "cornerstone of British colonial policy" (Lamothe, 1977, p. 86), were often used to impose physical, emotional and psychological damage on the indigenous communities of Canada in an effort to strip indigenous communities, including the Dene, of their beliefs and assimilate them into White British culture. Through it all, the Dene have maintained the desire for their children to be educated in a way that marries their traditional knowledges with the acquisition of skills such as literacy that will benefit them in the world they will enter beyond formal schooling.

Another indigenous community existing in Canada as well as the northern, midwestern United States is the Ojibwe. As of 2012, the Ojibwe had adopted a partnership between their White Earth Reservation Head Start Program and the University of Minnesota Department of Curriculum and Instruction, which effectively blends Ojibwe indigenous knowledge with science-based learning (Mason et al., 2012). Some in the learning community acknowledge the deficit-based beliefs with which many White teachers enter teacher/student relationships with indigenous children and that indigenous students face an uphill battle when they encounter teachers who fail to recognize their cultural values in the classroom. As such, strategists in the partnership sought the culturally relevant pedagogy of Gloria Ladson-Billings (1999, 2009). Together, the community made the intentional choice to focus on early childhood education spaces, and Headstart specifically, because of the well-documented influence the program has had on positive social-emotional growth. The partnership produced a space where children were able to connect with the land, where Objibwe language acquisition and preservation was prioritized and where teachers received regular support and professional development.

The United States

It is uncommon to have conversations about education in the United States without referencing the influence of John Dewey. What is relevant to the topic of global education is his challenge to the widely held beliefs of the time about who formal schooling was for. Rather than quality education being the domain of the elite, Dewey saw it as an opportunity to help all children understand their relationship to their world and to slowly expose them to more and more of that relationship as they developed in age-appropriate ways (Winsor, 1977). Through his work we begin to see an awareness in mainstream school environments in the United States of the benefits of providing experiences for young children to be connected to the world around them.

Piaget picks this theory up and extends it with the Interactionist position, correctly identifying the child as "a philosopher or a scientist – as an experimenter acquiring data from personal experience, and using that data to make sense of the world" (Winsor, 1977, p. 19). Here, the child is not a passive observer but an active participant in their world. It is their experience with this world, and others in it, that provides them with an awareness of differing viewpoints early in life. The Developmental Interaction Approach, which sprang from Dewey and Piaget as well as "progressive experimenters" like Lucy Sprague Mitchell, saw the direct relationship between the child's development process and their experience with the world around them. Here the child is constantly wondering about, making sense of and engaging with their various natural and social communities. It is a relationship through which they simultaneously define themselves and the world around them (Cuffaro, 1977).

When talking about the relationship between the world and the young child's understanding of themselves, it is important that the work of Derrick Bell and Gloria Ladson-Billings is always informing the conversation about global education. Ladson-Billings and Bell (1999) championed the field of Critical Race Theory (CRT) and define the philosophy as "a form of scholarship… that challenges the universality of white experience as the authoritative standard…" (p. 215). This theory interrupts commonly held practices in education (including within our early childhood spaces) that accept White western culture as the default, which has the impact of consistently silencing the voices of the marginalized and their family's and community's traditions and ways of being.

CRT relies on the storytelling traditions of Black and Brown communities to truly understand "their experiences and how those experiences may represent confirmation or counter knowledge of the way society works" (Ladson-Billings & Bell, 1999, p. 219). In other words, listening to the lived realities of people of color provides alternative stories which are equally true, valid and beneficial in early childhood spaces. This is useful in two primary ways. If these funds of knowledge are familiar and actively incorporated into the day-to-day life of early childhood programs, children see themselves reflected, thereby validating them and contributing to a feeling of connectedness. If they are not familiar, children are exposed early to points of view and ways of understanding the world outside of their own and gain practice in navigating and appreciating new perspectives. Those who challenge CRT often do so out of a sense of panic because they themselves have never experienced (and therefore have a low tolerance for) spaces where multiple identities and lived realities are properly honored and valued. It can feel disorienting and threatening when a perspective outside of our own is given equal attention to ours if all we've known is a world that centers our perspective of the world.

The work of anti-colonial theorists (Childs & Williams, 1997; Wane, 2008) in early education is also relevant to the conversation. Educational colonialism is an ongoing colonizing of the minds of children during which the child learns that they (and their current lived reality as well as their past) are welcomed only in limited geographic, social and emotional spaces. According to Childs and Williams, teaching that is anti-colonial relies on educating within a context that acknowledges that colonialism exists in the present as an ongoing phenomenon. It follows that a curriculum that is global in scope and speaks to the various histories, cultures and lived realities of people from historically marginalized communities is most effective when it provides perspectives which challenge the unique type of colonialism present in more traditional classroom settings and referred to by Ladson-Billings (2009) as the White supremacist master script. Teachers and communities are both anti-colonial and global when they seek to replace the current script with one that empowers all of their children, equally. The practice of global citizenship, defined in the next chapter, speaks to this effort directly.

While the strategies and specific cultural indicators may be vastly different, a shared goal of most societies when raising their very young is to equip them for a world that they can navigate successfully using tools that are familiar to the community. Reflecting on the idea of preparing the child, Charlotte Winsor (1977) noted that the goal, ultimately, is "to provide experience and content so that the child may become a knowing person in a knowable world" (p. 40). Recognized. Valued. Prepared. In the explicit and more subtle ways, all of the communities in this chapter enact some form of community-based education as a strategy for preparing the child for the world that they will inherit.

References

Abu-Saad, I., & Champagne, D. (Eds.) (2006). *Indigenous education and empowerment: International perspectives.* Altamira Press.

Almunajjed, M. (1997). *Women in Saudi Arabia today.* St. Martin's Press.

Aslan, E. (2020). *Migration, religion and early childhood education.* Springer Publications.

Berkey, J. (1992). *The transmission of knowledge in medieval Cairo: A social history of Islamic education*. Princeton University Press.

Childs, P., & Williams, P. (1997). *Introduction to postcolonial theory*. Prentice Hall.

Cuffaro, H. (1977). The developmental interaction approach. In B. Boegehold, H. Cuffaro, W. Hooks, & G. Klopf (Eds.), *Education before five* (pp. 45–53). Bank Street College of Education.

Daily, M., & Thompson, J. (2004). *The early childhood movement in Jamaica: Building blocks for the future*. Chalkboard Press.

Downs, L. (2002). *Childhood in the promised land: Working class movements and colones de vacances in France 1880–1960*. Duke University Press.

Duke, B (2009). *The history of modern Japanese education: Constructing the national school system, 1872–1890*. Rutgers University Press.

Ebrahim, H. B., Okwany, A., & Barry, O. (Eds.) (2019). *Early childhood care and education at the margins: African perspectives on birth to three*. Routledge.

Ensor, M. (2012). *African childhoods: Education, development, and peacebuilding, and the youngest continent*. Palgrave Macmillan.

Kamusiine, A. (2019). Early childhood care narratives of young mothers in Uganda. In H. B. Ebrahim, A. Okwany, & O. Barry (Eds.), *Early childhood care and education at the margins: African perspectives on birth to three* (pp. 102–117). Routledge.

Ladson-Billings, G. (1999). Preparing teachers for diverse student population: A critical race theory perspective. *Review of Research in Education, 24*, 211–247.

Ladson-Billings, G. (2009). *The dreamkeepers: Successful teachers of African American children*. Jossey-Bass.

Lamothe, R. (1977). Statement to the Mackenzie Valley Pipeline Inquiry. In M. Watkins (Ed.), *Dene Nation: The colony within* (pp. 10–11, 86). University of Toronto Press.

Langdon, S. (2013). Children as learners and producers in early Greece. In J. E. Grubbs & T. Parkin (Eds.), *Childhood and education in the classical world* (pp. 172–194). Oxford University Press.

Mason, A., Dubosarsky, M., Roehrig, G., Farley, M., Carlson, S., & Murphy, B. (2012). Ah neen dush: Harnessing collective wisdom to create culturally relevant science experiences in pre-k classrooms. In S. Gregory (Ed), *Voices of Native American educators: Integrating history, culture, and language to improve learning outcomes for Native American Students* (pp. 79–98). Lexington Books.

Mfum-Mensah, O. (2017). *Education, social progress and marginalized children in sub-Saharan Africa: Historical antecedents and contemporary challenges*. Lexington Books.

Qureshi, I. (1975). *Education in Pakistan: An inquiry into objectives and achievements*. Ma'Aref Ltd.

Roopnarine, J., & Brown, J. (Eds.) (1997). *Caribbean families: Diversity among ethnic groups*. Abex Publishing.

Schwartzman, S. (Ed.) (2015). *Education in South America*. Bloomsbury.

Swaminathan, M. (Ed.) (1998). *The first five years: A critical perspective on early care and education in India*. SAGE Publications.

Wane, N. (2008). Mapping the field of indigenous knowledges in anti-colonial discourse: A transformative journey in education. *Race Ethnicity and Education, 11*(2), 183–197.

Williams, J. (2013). The socialization of Roman children. In J. E. Grubbs & T. Parkin (Eds.), *Childhood and education in the classical world* (pp. 264–285). Oxford University Press.

Winsor, C. (1977). The progressive movement. In B. Boegehold, H. Cuffaro, W. Hooks, & G. Klopf (Eds.), *Education before five* (pp. 19–40). Bank Street College of Education.

Zingzhi, T. (2016). *The transformation of Chinese traditional education: Selected papers by Tao Xingzhi on education*. Brill Publications.

What is Global Citizenship?

Because the terms *global citizen* and *global citizenship education* are used so regularly throughout this book it may be useful to offer a few definitions of the terms. At the virtual summit of the Global Education Benchmark Group in August 2020, twenty different Directors of Global Education across the country defined global citizenship in twenty different ways. That is the beauty and also the challenge of the work. For the sake of the conversation, it's useful to share some of the definitions that have informed the work over the years.

Lagos (2002) defines global citizenship as unlimited by such things as space and time and allows a state of being that "travels [across] these various layers or boundaries and somehow still makes sense of the world" (p. 9). Tsolidis (2002) builds on this by defining global citizenship as "the relationship the individual can establish with a community which is conceptualized as transcending the local and indeed the national" (p. 216). Here, community is broadly defined and boundaries are elastic rather than static. Hicks (2003) references Richardson's exploration of the field with the assertion that the relationship between a community and the world cannot be effective unless it assumes that all those involved are capable of creating a system rooted in empowerment and equality and are eager to resist educational trends that simply reinforce inequality. Rapoport (2009) provides the definition that I am most drawn to. Referencing McIntosh, the author defines global citizenship as the "habits of mind, heart, body and soul that have to do with working for and preserving a network of relationships and connections across lines of difference and distinctness, while keeping and deepening a sense of one's own identity and integrity" (p. 93). I favor

DOI: 10.4324/9781003005186-5

this definition because it implies that one does not have to give up their personal, cultural or community-based identity to develop relationships with and appreciation for others. Here, the successful global citizen does two things simultaneously. They possess a deep love for and affinity towards their own identified community and they succeed in understanding that they are a part of a larger, global community with members whose lives and perspectives are just as rich, complex and valued as their own.

All of this can be done, as Tsolidis explains, while operating from the perspective that, though occupying individual identities, all are members of the same community. It is only from this place that both effective community building and global cooperation can be achieved. For this reason, it is crucial that the practice of global citizenship begins early in a child's life.

At this point, it may be important to note the subtleties between *multicultural* education and *global citizenship* education. There is a beauty in multicultural education when it is done right. In "A new childhood social studies curriculum for a new generation of citizenship" in 2009's *International Journal of Children's Rights*, vol. 17, Camicia and Saaveda name multicultural education as a form of curriculum that "promotes social justice… When multiple cultural perspectives are valued in the curriculum, the curriculum can be responsive and relevant to the needs of all students" (p. 505). This blend of cultural experience and the intentional use of that experience to promote equity in the classroom has the potential to inspire inquiry and radical change to an existing structure while validating the lived experiences of all of its students. James A. Banks (2007) offers a rubric for healthy and effective multicultural education made up of several "dimensions" including content integration, prejudice reduction, equity pedagogy and empowering school culture. Multicultural education has the potential to be an extraordinary tool of practice for families, teachers and children not only if it is effectively integrated into the life of the school, but if it is used intentionally to engage adults as well as children in explorations of biases and prejudices and if it actually empowers disempowered children and communities by elevating their voices and experiences consistently.

Unfortunately, the reality often looks very different. A problem that many schools run into is that they often fail to effectively incorporate this type of social justice-oriented multiculturalism actively and consistently into the curriculum and daily life of their classrooms. Teachers in American schools tend to be chronically overworked, criminally underpaid (Reilly,

2018) and often lack the professional support necessary to enact meaningful, personalized and fully integrated multicultural curricula. Under these conditions, what children often receive instead is a watered-down highlight reel relegated to a few days out of the year rather than a fully infused day-to-day engagement with a variety of perspectives that regularly validate *and* stretch their own identities and perspectives.

In a typical school year at one of my very first teaching assignments, one day featured a forty-minute assembly for Diwali, another, a morning meeting about Kwanzaa, the story of Hanukkah during lunch on another day, and so on. Well-meaning and correctly identified on the calendar as these events were, they were located within a school curriculum that utilized an otherwise Euro-centric, middle class identity in every other part of the day and every other day of the school year. This meant that the art supplies and ways of making art were inspired primarily by the European (and more specifically, the Flemish, German and Spanish) masters. The vast majority of books visible and on the shelves were written by White writers and featured White protagonists. The layout and furniture in the rooms reflected American minimalist design made popular in the 1950s during the post-war suburban boom (in other words, lacking both color and design diversity). Parent Association meeting agendas revolved around benefit planning and play date schedules but never around self-reflection or strategies for talking to children (or among themselves) about identity. Administrators rarely examined the possibilities of engagement with the communities surrounding the preschool. And so on...

Some would say that this type of school environment sends a message that runs counter to early education's purpose. It could be argued that if early childhood education in the United States is meant to prepare young children for the world that they will enter beyond the classroom (with its resistance to both respect for historically marginalized identities and stewardship and communal problem solving), this type of education fulfills its purpose in profoundly effective ways. To the White children I encountered, the message received was that their lives and the lives of people who looked like them were meant to be centered and to take up more space. They were meant to see themselves reflected everywhere. Who they were and the various ways that they interpreted the world were of primary importance. In this same environment, the message to children of color was that their lives were meant to be limited to the margins. Their voices were less often acknowledged. Who they were and what they desired was only valuable

What is Global Citizenship?

as it related to how they diversified and improved the vibrancy and quality of life of their White peers.

Often these type of multicultural curricula are enacted in ways that perpetuate a disconnected relationship with the world. It is me-centered (Figure 3.1) and tends to have an absence of experiences that engage children in the practice of authentic community. Although decontextualized moments (for instance, a holiday or a type of food) may be explored, at no point is the child challenged to genuinely consider the world from the point of view of someone else through prolonged engagement. What happens is that the child begins to understand the experiences of others as important only in so much as they benefit their own.

Global citizenship education answers this by engaging in the search not only for commonalities but, also, for mutual value. It intentionally facilitates an interconnected relationship with the world (Figure 3.2) where our whole selves meet the whole selves of others and where one's value is undiminished by the presence and value of others.

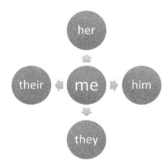

Figure 3.1 Multicultural education

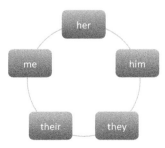

Figure 3.2 Global citizenship education

Development, Early Education and Global Citizenship Education

One of the ways that it does this is by actively normalizing an awareness of our identities within a global context. Subedi (2010) elaborates on this by noting that effective global education highlights the need to teach in ways that embody the histories, traditions and cultures represented in our classrooms as well as others not necessarily represented within our cultural or national borders. This leap, from the personal to the global, is the context within which young children begin to gain a sense of what it means to occupy community that is structured in ways that provide equal space for their peers', as well as their own, whole selves. In these spaces, children grow up to be adults who have had considerable practice living in a world where fewer are at the margins and "normal" is an environment where all can be heard, acknowledged and honored. Instead of panic and alarm, these adults experience a sense of normalcy when the narratives of others are properly acknowledged.

This "normal", taught early in life, has the potential to destabilize American hypernationalism as we know it. It is possible for children to experience early learning environments that achieve the goal of teaching them the skill of reaching across boundaries of difference (both geographical and philosophical) with mutual respect and appreciation from an early age. What I am suggesting is that only when multicultural education is enacted as global citizenship practice does it become a logical and effective strategy for equipping young children with the tools necessary to disrupt a country and a world inundated with division and soul-destroying inequities.

As will be seen, strategies for teaching global citizenship are widely varied but the general motivation for doing so is fairly consistent. Tsolidis (2002) notes, "specific cultures are no longer confined to defined communities or contained by national boundaries" (p. 216). In order to operate in this increasingly globalized world, children must learn from an early age how to move about among others who occupy different cultural, ethnic, personal and linguistic spaces. Camicia and Saavedra (2009) suggest an ongoing conversation about globalization that they deem as essential to the development of young children. Referring to Banks, the authors agree that an education that is both multicultural and global must be created in such a way that children, regardless of age, can learn about the world *and* take responsibility for effecting positive change in that world. Rejecting traditional models of social studies that rely on students only being capable

40

of conceptualizing their own personal experiences and those within their immediate surroundings as complex and impactful, they advocate for a thematic approach that locates the child at the center of a series of concentric circles. Children must first learn about the value that they innately possess within themselves and then about their relationship to the people and environments around them in ever-widening ways until they have a firm and well-rounded understanding that, at any given time, they exist within multiple spheres of community alongside many different people, both local and global.

Yet another value of teaching global citizenship is the embedded practice of developing intimate rather than superficial relationships beyond our identified boundaries. In his article, "Seeking a curricular soul", former director of the Department of Social Studies at Teachers College, Columbia, William Gaudelli (2010), lays out a strategy for developing a practice of relationship building that reaches across boundaries towards others as a means of establishing genuine connection:

> when we exhort students to care about the world, think globally, be global citizens, these calls ring hollow unless we have engaged them in a full explanation of what it means to care, to love, to befriend, to be intimate.
>
> (p. 150)

Gaudelli's concept of globally minded students adds depth to the existing literature on the topic and drives home the necessity of grounding the work in personal relationships.

This is the story of two very different preschools. One is informed by an intentionally Pan-Africanist curriculum and inspired by a mother's search for more inclusive educational choices for her own young children in the heart of a beloved New York City neighborhood gentrifying at a break-neck pace. The other is at the intersection of Hawaiian tradition, independent school culture and a uniquely Italian, community-based philosophy for educating children. Both are extraordinary examples of early childhood global citizenship education in practice. I chose these two schools, Little Sun People, Inc., in the Bedford-Stuyvesant neighborhood of Brooklyn, NY and Mid-Pacific Institute Preschool, on the island of Oahu, HA, because although on paper, their demographics, geographic location and philosophies are vastly different, when we examine their creation, curricula, what their children believe about themselves and others and the teaching strategies of their educators, we begin to see, within both, the early cultivation of engaged global citizens.

References

Banks, J. A. (2007). *Educating citizens in a multicultural society*. Teachers College Press.

Camicia, S., & Saavedra, C. (2009). A new childhood social studies curriculum for a new generation of citizenship. *International Journal of Children's Rights, 17*, 501–517.

Gaudelli, W. (2010). Seeking a curricular soul: Moving global education in space/place, with intimacy, and toward aesthetic experience. In B. Subedi (Ed.), *Critical global perspectives: Rethinking knowledge about global societies* (pp. 143–160). Information Age Publishing, Inc.

Gaudelli, W. (2003). *World class: Teaching and learning in global times*. Lawrence Erlbaum Associates, Inc., Publishers.

Hicks, D. (2003). Thirty years of global education: A reminder of key principles and precedents. *Educational Review, 55*(3), 265–275.

Lagos, T. (2002). *Global citizenship – Towards a definition*. The Global Citizenship Project. The University of Washington Center for Communication and Civic Engagement.

Rapoport, A. (2009). A forgotten concept: Global citizenship education and state social studies standards. *The Journal of Social Studies Research, 33*(1), 91–112.

Reilly, K. (2018). https://time.com/longform/teaching-in-america

Subedi, B. (2010). *Critical global perspectives: Rethinking knowledge about global societies*. Information Age Publishing, Inc.

Tsolidis, G. (2002). How do we teach and learn in times when the notion of 'global citizenship' sounds like a cliché? *Journal of Research in International Education, 1*(213), 213–226.

PART

II

Global Citizenship Education in Practice
Little Sun People

Little Sun People
The Context of Community

Little Sun People is a four-classroom preschool housed in a lovingly converted warehouse in the predominantly African American, African, and Afro-Caribbean corner of the Bedford-Stuyvesant neighborhood of Brooklyn, New York. The area known as Brooklyn (and the greater New York area as a whole) was originally inhabited by the Lenape indigenous community, a subset of the people of the Delaware Nation which included the Nyack and the Canarsee tribes. *Lenapehoking*, as the region was known to the Lenape, has traditionally been home to wildlife such as wild-tailed deer, river otters, northern bald eagles, fox and coyote and its proximity to a large harbor and multiple rivers meant that local communities had access to rich bounties of oysters, porgies, bluefish and striped bass.

The Lenape community is matrilineal; children inherit and identify through their mother's clan and new families have traditionally lived with the bride's side of the family. Land was managed and passed down through her and women managed large tracts of cultivated earth where traditional crops of maize, squash and a variety of beans were staples in the community's diet. Men were generally responsible for hunting the abundant wildlife in the region as well as protecting the clan. Their successful relationship with the land around them meant that the community was one of the larger clans in the Northeast.

With the arrival of Dutch farmers seeking land across the river from the more populated Manhattan island, the Lenape community was almost completely decimated and most of the remaining community was pushed west and onto reservations by the Indian Removal Act of 1860. A series of smaller holdings were eventually incorporated by the Dutch into what is

DOI: 10.4324/9781003005186-7   45

Global Citizenship Education in Practice: Little Sun People

known today as Brooklyn in 1646 and was surrendered to the English in 1664. The town of Bedford, in the Northern-Central part of Brooklyn, was eventually named Bedford-Stuyvesant after the last Dutch governor of the colony and a city grid was completed in the 1860s although it remained mostly rural for several decades more.

Free Black communities existed throughout the United States in the first half of the 19th century although the official end of the enslavement of Black people would not come until 1865. New York's Free Black population was substantial and Weeksville, located on the border between Bedford-Suyvesant and the community of Crown Heights, was one such community (*The New York Times*, 2021). Made up of land purchased in 1838 by Black longshoreman James Weeks, the community was an exclusively African American enclave with its own school, churches, grocers, newspaper and an elder care facility. At its height, Weeksville included nearly 700 Black New Yorkers who, as landowners, provided much needed political power to the growing African American population in the north. A laser focus on self-determination and, in particular, control of the education their children received, was a signature feature in many Free communities and as the families in Weeksville eventually blended into the neighborhoods surrounding it, they brought this commitment with them.

The stately masonry townhomes that characterize Bedford-Stuyvesant today were largely built by German immigrants and bought by the growing German, Irish and English middle class. Today, these much sought-after homes are some of the most recognizable and expensive real estate in New York City and attract both independent buyers from all over the world as well as developers hoping to build around them and cash in on the recent influx of wealthier inhabitants. At the turn of the last century, however, significant communities of Jewish and Italian families began to inhabit the neighborhood as a result of the Williamsburg bridge connection between lower Manhattan and Brooklyn. Two decades later, immigrants from across the Caribbean began to settle in Brooklyn as well in search of economic opportunity and stability and the community remains strongly West Indian to this day.

Around this time, American Blacks had also been arriving from the southern states in the waves of the Great Migration to large northern cities such as Detroit, Chicago and New York hoping to find opportunities for economic advancement and a reprieve from racial violence. Many followed family and opportunity to Harlem, the Black enclave in Northern Manhattan which, at the time, was experiencing an extraordinary cultural

46

The Context of Community

renaissance and attracting the best of the country's intellectual and artistic minds. Reflecting on what the neighborhood meant to Blacks at the time, Ossie Davis opined, "…Harlem was home; was where we belonged; where we knew and were known in return; where we felt most alive…" (Davis & Dee, 2000, p. 65). By the 1930s Harlem's swelling population needed additional space and many set their sights on Brooklyn. In addition, with the ending of World War II, industrial plants, built to serve the war effort, began to close rapidly in the Midwest, driving Black families from that part of the country eastward, in search of jobs. Many of these families found themselves in Bedford-Stuyvesant. One of the greatest attractions of the growing community was the sense of independence, the seeds of which were planted by self-sustaining communities such as Weeksville, which brought with it safety and familiarity, recreated by those now distanced from their families in other parts of the country. Over the next three decades, Bedford-Stuyvesant's Black population grew to 85% of the population of the neighborhood.

It was through this swell that the community became a diasporic and unapologetic haven for a Black majority where community, cultural expression and pride shaped the day-to-day lives of adults and children alike (see Figures 4.1 and 4.2). Love (2019) defines these safe places where Black children are loved in their entirety in the context of community as their "homeplace". It is a space "where Black folx truly matter to each other, where

Figure 4.1 Children at Little Sun People dance during a performance

Figure 4.2 Bedford-Stuyvesant's stately townhouses are some of the most recognizable homes in the country

souls are nurtured, comforted, and fed… where White power and the damage done by it are healed by loving Blackness and restoring dignity" (p. 63).

Long-time community members describe Bedford-Stuyvesant of the 1940s through the 1980s as an intergenerational, culturally rich bubble that White Brooklynites largely avoided.

> The thing that we had that I loved the most was that you could hear music all the time. People would be talking and hanging out. The old people would be out. You just see Black people moving comfortably. The hair, the clothes, the confident feeling of being at home with your people. Laughing big. Spending time with each other. There was the warmth of community.
>
> (Fela Barclift)

Bedford-Stuyvesant and other Northern predominantly Black communities were not free from racism and danger, however. When an off-duty police officer shot and killed fifteen-year-old James Powell in Harlem in 1964, longstanding frustrations with New York City police brutality and the institutional racism that supported it could no longer be contained and erupted in violence for three nights both uptown and in Bed-Stuy. The resulting mobilization led to grassroots efforts on the community's part to protect itself and voice its concerns about the disempowerment it faced. Lack of government investment, racist housing practices and the lack of policy to prevent it (particularly a predatory gentrification that has gripped the neighborhood for the better part of the last four decades), and the closing or decline of several large job providers, including the Brooklyn Naval Yard and the Sheffield Farms Milk Bottling Plant, have also threatened to rupture the close-knit extended family feel of the neighborhood over the years.

What has remained a constant presence is the resilience the community prides itself on, even in the most weathering of years, and the joy of finding itself still intact and full of the determination necessary to carry on. One manifestation of that determination has been the development of the Bedford-Stuyvesant Community Restoration Corporation (see Figure 4.3), or simply Restoration as it's known in the neighborhood.

Today Restoration "relentlessly pursues strategies to close gaps in family and community wealth to ensure all families in central Brooklyn are prosperous and healthy" (restorationplaza.org). To date, the organization is responsible for renovating over 2000 homes and investing 375 million dollars into the community. Restoration Plaza, at the intersection of Fulton and New York Avenues, houses shops, office and event space and a theater in the former Sheffield Farms Milk Bottling Plant and is a thriving arts and community space. Little Sun People Preschool lives adjacent to the Plaza on Herkimer Street, a fitting location for a preschool so deeply devoted to the community it serves and a natural choice for its creator, Fela Barclift.

Figure 4.3 Restoration Plaza, one of Bedford-Stuyvesant's cultural and artistic hubs

Fela Barclift and the Creation of a School of Resistance

Mama Fela, a title afforded to her and all women at Little Sun People (men are referred to as "Baba") referencing the structures of honor towards adults found in numerous communities of color across the world, was not planning on being a teacher. Growing up, she saw few teachers that she desired to emulate. Her own educators made her feel invisible and the curricula she encountered left her feeling "ashamed. And robbed". As an African American woman, she did not see herself or the community she identified with reflected in her textbooks, which from an early age had been the Black/African American community of Bedford-Stuyvesant and also the global Black community occupying a large portion of the world outside of the United States. When she did, the images she received were condescending and, consistently, historically inaccurate.

This is not a unique experience. Subedi (2010) provides an analysis of world history textbooks that found that "1) Third World countries were underrepresented in textbooks, 2) there was no mention of major Third World historical events, 3) emphasis was placed on the benefits of European imperialism and 4) reports on current conditions of Third World countries depicted only bleak conditions" (p. 136). This experience with an education that depicted people of color across the world as generally unsuccessful at life and dependent on [wealthy] European influence for peace, stability and culture has had deteriorating effects on the positive self-image of students of African heritage. Over a decade since the publication of Subedi's work, the quality of educational material for young students has improved only marginally.

Hidden curricula are also at play in public schools in densely populated "urban areas" around the country that make different types of education available to different socio-economic demographics of students (Anyon, 1980). Traditionally, opportunities to develop the knowledge and skills leading to social power (skills such as curiosity, confidence, ownership of ideas and analytical thinking) are made available in affluent and elite schools and actively withheld in schools serving predominantly working class and middle class communities. It has been theorized that to deny children from economically suppressed communities the practice of independence, of thinking critically and of challenging dominant beliefs, has

The Context of Community

been an effective strategy for training them to remain a subjected class. For Mama Fela, it was a discouraging and demoralizing experience.

What she did see all around her were civil rights attorneys and activists effectively resisting acceptance of a substandard way of living and she determined to go into a career in law. It was around this time, in the late 1960s, that she became involved in the Pan-Africanist movement whose goal is the solidarity and self-actualization of the African diaspora across the world. A world-wide lineage, from Angola's Queen Nzinga to Jamaican-born Marcus Garvey to Ghana's first democratically elected president, Kwame Nkrumah to Trinidadian-American Stokely Carmichael (Later Kwame Ture) and beyond, has led the Pan-Africanist movement through many iterations. As such, education steeped in this philosophy of unity across cultures and geographic lines is, by its nature, global in scope. Organizations such as the African American Teachers Association and the EAST, a multi-functioning community arts and education collective based in Bedford-Stuyvesant, were the result of the Pan-Africanist influence.

Invited to teach at the now-closed Uhuru Sasa (Freedom Now) School in 1970, Mama Fela found a space to blend her commitment to her community with her desire to infuse positive self-esteem into the lives of young children in ways that she and her peers had not had access to. Teaching became a way of seeing and doing and knowing, exploring together and learning from each other in a collaborative process with her students that encouraged both questioning of and pride in their world as well as constant opportunities to understand that world from the varying perspectives of their peers in the global community. It was here that Mama Fela identified a fundamental problem that would guide her vision.

> I was teaching girls who were eight, nine, ten, but I could see I was putting something on top of something they had already learned. The messages they receive about invalidation are constant. My goal is to start when they're babies and [show them] that they're members of a global community. We stare at each other across this divide but we are each other. The human race is a cooperative.

A few years later, as the mother of two small children, her strategy was put to the test. The childcare options available to Mama Fela in the neighborhood were abysmal. By the time her daughter was school age, Uhuru Sasa had closed and she could not find an early education space where

51

she felt her child would see herself not just reflected in, but uplifted by, the curriculum. Instead, Barclift opted to finish her degree and home school her children. By taking in a small number of other community children and teaching them alongside her own, she effectively made the first floor of her brownstone home into a family child care program. Family Child Care is arguably the oldest type of early education in the United States and ranges from informal care, usually run by a trusted member of the community without formal credentials, to formal Family and Group Family Child Care programs. These programs are rooted in community, providing early education as well as necessary and personalized care to families such as flexible hours for parents with difficult work schedules, connections to community resources providing such necessities as food, housing and clothes and a stable, familiar base for children to begin their lives outside of their family home while staying firmly rooted in their community. Sometimes these care programs are regulated by the Department of Health and The Office of Children and Family Services and may receive support from teachers unions as well as local family child care networks. Mama Fela's program mirrored these programs in that her primary objective was to provide quality early childhood care and education that reflected the cultural and community needs of the families that she served.

Four years later, realizing that she was outgrowing the space, Mama Fela moved the program to Restoration Plaza where she and dedicated members of the community, educators, artists and others set out to build a personalized and responsive program for young children in the neighborhood. It was an empowered decision which, over the years, has led to the multi-classroom program that Little Sun People is today.

Through her work, Mama Fela contributes to a long lineage of Black women utilizing teaching not only as a way of shaping their personal lives but also as a tool to help steer the community in the midst of school systems hindered by racism, sexism and socio-economic exclusion (Dingus, 2008). This lineage within the United States extends at least as far back as Reconstruction, a period when the formally enslaved began to exercise their right to self-determination through teaching in, and the maintenance of, their own schools while resisting the help of outside influences. For the last century and a half, African American communities have gathered what little income they could spare and relied on community skill to construct buildings from the ground up when local governments refused to provide the money or manpower (Anderson, 1988). In the same way, Mama Fela utilized the skills within her

The Context of Community

community to realize her vision. Educators assisted in building the curriculum. Artists painted murals of diasporic heroes. Neighbors and friends colored in picture books that featured only White children when good representation could not be found in bookstores. Her chess, violin, drum and dance teachers, yoga instructor and Swahili expert have all been Black and Brown educators from the surrounding communities. Children see themselves and their cultures reflected back to them everywhere they look, which often stands in stark contrast to their experience outside of the community.

Reflecting on her own early experiences of having Black teachers, bell hooks (1994) describes how this teaching, for Black people, has always been political and anti-racist. Less a teaching style, what Mama Fela and her team bring into the classroom is direct action taken to speak back to educational and social injustices that they themselves have lived. Love describes this strategy as Abolitionist Teaching; a means of resistance "through teachers who work in solidarity with their schools' community to achieve incremental changes in their classrooms and schools for students in the present day, while simultaneously freedom dreaming and vigorously creating a vision for what schools will be" (p. 89).

The School

A bright bulletin board featuring the school's mission, a prayer of gratitude, announcements and school and community resources greets visitors upon entry into the building. In the main space, classrooms are divided by cubbies, bookcases and dramatic play structures instead of walls. There are, on nearly every surface, colorful posters of historical heroes from each continent. Children's artwork and statements of affirmation dot surfaces. The cement floor is covered with colorful carpeting that helps to designate the various areas of the classrooms (see Figure 4.4). Images of family, in all of their iterations, smile back at children who lovingly touch them and refer to them often.

The classrooms themselves are tightly packed with materials, tables, cubbies and storage spaces. There are separate, smaller rooms at the back of the preschool in addition to a small kitchen, the director's office and an administrative office. The teachers use the smaller classrooms for dance, music and other small group activities. The building, being a former warehouse, is lit mostly with artificial light.

Figure 4.4 (a) The Zulu Fouriors room with Kente cloth, family photos, natural plants and children's artwork on every surface. (b) The 2020 Little Sun People Kwanzaa table

The preschool enrolls approximately fifty-six children (eighty-five including an active afterschool program) between the ages of two and five years old and employs ten full time teachers, auxiliary staff and administrative personnel. The children come from a mixture of working class and middle class families, predominantly living in Bedford-Stuyvesant but also from across the New York area, who play an integral role in the life of the school. The school is predominantly African American and Afro-Caribbean with several families from continental Africa who attend also. Occasionally, White families will enroll their children as well and Mama Fela has stated explicitly that the program has always been open to all, regardless of racial or ethnic background. The life of the school is a joint effort between the teachers and families with the school building being a second home to families and their children. "They live here. We joke with them that we can't get them out. They socialize, plan, set up shop and make things happen right here", Mama Fela says. Numerous studies have been done that show that family involvement improves the experience of young children in their earliest educational settings (Cohen & Anders, 2020; Knopf & Swick, 2008; Souto-Manning, 2006, etc.). For the teams at Little Sun People, having families involved is a natural extension of how multi-generational community operates effectively.

Of the historical trends within American schools, Subedi (2010) notes that young children's training to be uncritical of what it means to be an

The Context of Community

American is one of the most damaging. Embedded in what it means to be American is often a worldview that centralizes a western perspective. Gaudelli (2003) effectively synthesizes this worldview by naming it as a dichotomous relationship between those who have agency and write their own history and those who have no agency and about whom history is written. Little Sun People subverts this relationship regularly by constructing a definition of self and citizenship that elevates both the child's immediate community and the wider world of the African diaspora.

> Praise the Red, the Black and the Green
> The brothers and sisters are being redeemed
> Why don't you open up your eyes and see
> We're on our way to being free!
> (Umoja Pledge Flag Song sung by children at Little Sun People)

Through their participation in the life of the preschool, influenced by the Pan-Africanist movement, children come to understand themselves as members of both and learn the habit of applying value to both.

A typical day in the four-year-old class, known as the Zulu Fouriors, begins before 8 am. Teachers are present and ready to receive early drop-offs. As children arrive, both they and their parents sign in. In the early morning, the classes usually combine and older children have the opportunity to play with their younger peers. Arrival is staggered but most children are in by 9:00 am when the classes separate and breakfast is provided with children serving themselves. Movement time typically happens after breakfast to "get some of the wiggles out". Afterwards, children sit down for morning meeting and the teachers, Mama Aaliyah, Mama Nikia and Mama Linda, guide them through a topic of discussion, including a turn and talk, sometimes based on a project they have been working on. Storytime often happens during this time as well. Nearly every day that the weather permits, the children go outside in groups with Mama Linda staying behind to work with children on small group activities until it is their turn outside. A portion of each day is also given over to Swahili, dance or martial arts. Before lunch, the children remove their shoes, find their resting mats and lay them throughout the classroom. Lunch is always eaten together between 12:00 and 1:00 and naptime is between 1:00 and 3:00 pm, a significant amount of time but necessary given the children's always busy mornings. When they wake, mats are put away and a snack is served. Some

Reflection

Describe your community. What makes it unique? Do you feel at home in it?

What is the history of your community?

Who are the culture bearers (the individuals or organizations that carry on the community's traditions and educate others about its history and influence) in your community?

What options for early childhood education are available in your community? How are they influenced by the neighborhood, families and cultures that they serve?

The Context of Community

children leave at 3:30, while others stay until the end of the day at 6:00 pm. Typically, the afternoon is their time and children can choose an activity or spend time with friends from other classrooms again.

I first encountered Little Sun People on the recommendation of a colleague in my third year of my graduate work while searching for preschools to observe that had global curricula. My first email to Mama Fela was responded to almost immediately and we commenced to a virtual exchange that reminded me more of a conversation between a mentor and mentee than between strangers who happened to be in the same field. I began to observe in the spring of 2014, ultimately taking part in the community as a participant observer and the school became the primary point of reference for my dissertation the following year. The children in the Zulu Fouriors classroom eventually grew accustomed to my being there every Monday morning and the teachers patiently walked me through their curriculum and process.

References

Anderson, J. (1988). *The education of blacks in the south, 1860–1935*. The University of North Carolina Press.

Anyon, J. (1980). Social class and the hidden curriculum of work. *Journal of Education, 6162*(1), 67–93.

Cohen, F., & Anders, Y. (2020). Family involvement in early childhood education and care and its effects on the socio-emotional and language skills of 3-year-old children. *School Effectiveness and School Improvement, 31*(1), 125–142.

Davis, O., & Dee, R. (2000) *With Ossie and Ruby: In this life together*. HarperCollins.

Dingus, J. (2008). 'Our family business was education': Professional socialization among intergenerational African-American teaching families. *International Journal of Qualitative Studies in Education, 21*(6), 605–626.

Gaudelli, W. (2003). *World class: Teaching and learning in global times*. Lawrence Erlbaum Associates, Inc., Publishers.

hooks, b. (1994). *Teaching to transgress: Education as the practice of freedom*. Routledge.

Knopf, H., & Swick, K. (2008). Using our understanding of families to strengthen family involvement. *Early Childhood Education Journal, 35,* 419–427.

Love, B. (2019). *We want to do more than survive: Abolitionist teaching and the pursuit of educational freedom.* Beacon Press.

The New York Times. (2021). www.nytimes.com/2021/04/06/arts/design/save-weeksville-cig.html

Restoration Plaza. www.restorationplaza.org

Souto-Manning, M. (2006). Teachers' beliefs about parent and family involvement: Rethinking our family involvement paradigm. *Early Childhood Education Journal, 34*(2), 187–193.

Subedi, B. (2010). *Critical global perspectives: Rethinking knowledge about global societies.* Information Age Publishing, Inc.

The Garvey School. www.thegarveyschool.org

Weeksville. www.weeksvillesociety.org

Little Sun People
Lessons in Power

Merriam-Webster defines "power" as "the ability or right to control people or things… a person or organization that has a lot of control and influence over other people or organizations" (www.merriam-webster.com). The Oxford Dictionary defines "power" as "The capacity or ability to direct or influence the behavior of others or the course of events" (www. oxforddictionaries.com). An understanding of power as a tool for African American children's empowerment may be closer to this second definition of the term: the ability to influence the world around them for their benefit. Lessons in Power are experiences that teach children about their ability to influence their environment in ways that are influential to their happiness while simultaneously subverting negative messages about themselves and their communities. Of the multi-dimensional definition that Watts (2013) offers for "power", one section is particularly relevant. It is "the capacity to achieve ones aims" (p. 59).

Within the context of global citizenship, this definition of power is particularly poignant. When teachers at Little Sun People are working to teach their children that they are part of a global community that is large, vibrant and valuable, an important component at work is children's understanding of their ability to influence that community and reach their goals through that influence. Developmentally, this goal is aligned with the child's newly discovered awareness of the impact that they have on the world around them. "Power" is gained at Little Sun People as the result of messages children receive about their ability to be heard, acknowledged, responded to and loved in ways that centralize their experiences. The preschool achieves this in a few key ways.

DOI: 10.4324/9781003005186-8

Validation

Validation is an act of seeing. When we are seen (and heard and understood) we learn that our perspective is valued right where we are. In the Zulu Fouriors classroom, validation shows up in specific as well as in more generalized ways. Specifically, it is evident in the acknowledging and normalizing of the day-to-day feelings and experiences of children in the school. Mama Aaliyah, the lead teacher in the room, enjoys reading to the children and engaging them in conversations about what they see and feel during story time. In a small group conversation about a book with a boy who was labeled "naughty", a child reflected, "I go hyper sometimes". Mama Aaliyah paused the story to respond that "we all go hyper sometimes". After a beat, the child smiled and Mama Aaliyah continued. Afterwards, Mama Aaliyah explained that the child was in fact a very active child and that she and his mother had been in ongoing conversation about how best to support him. Armed with a plan, Mama Aaliyah acknowledged him, and his feelings in the moment, each time she could. In this simple exchange the child had a moment of self-reflection that his teacher took time to validate with her own. In letting him know that she too experienced a similar sensation, the teacher took a mildly negative statement and reframed it as normal and free of judgment.

Another specific example of validation occurred during afternoon yoga. The instructor, Mama Barabi, spent the hour teaching the children how to play a game called "toe-ga" where a pile of multi-colored pompoms was placed in the center of the circle and children were given the task of picking them up using only their toes. While playing, one child became frustrated and said "I can't do it". The teacher next to him, who normally teaches in another class, said "Yes you can, you gotta curl your toes. Pick it up like this" and modeled the slow, steady movement necessary to pick the soft piece up by catching it between her big toe and the ball of her foot. After a few failed attempts, the child succeeded in picking it up and held it up between his toes for the teacher to see, who clapped excitedly.

With a full daily classroom schedule, Mama Aaliyah uses validation to navigate and support children's actions in ways that take the group from activity to activity as smoothly as possible. When she wants the children to practice healthy and safe behavior in a particular way, she utilizes positive reinforcement, drawing attention to the actions of one child for the other children to notice and use as example.

"Ok, let me see who's ready. Ok, J, I love it. J is ready!"

In this way, she validates J's efforts, reinforces the value of the behavior she desires from all of her students from a strength-based perspective and gives them a concrete example to follow for moving effectively throughout the physical space.

> Why is it important to validate children's experiences? How do you validate the feelings and experiences of children in your classroom/life?

Validation shows up more generally at Little Sun People in the elevation of African diasporic history and tradition, generally meant as any cultural experience or tradition that has its roots in Africa (see Figure 5.1). Teachers create an atmosphere where students understand that the cultural experiences that they learn about are a part of their own heritage as opposed to something separate and distant from their lived reality. While it's used to refer to all non-Europeans in a general sense, "African heritage" is also used to describe several African cultures specifically. The intentional relationship that is messaged as occurring between the children and these cultures is a primary indicator of the focus on global community at Little Sun People. An example of this is the use of the collective "we" when asking questions about the people in books that are read.

Figure 5.1 Pan-African flags, recreated by children with acrylic paint, hang on the wall

Global Citizenship Education in Practice: Little Sun People

Teacher: So before we came… before our ancestors came to America, were we a part of different African cultures?
Children: Yes.
Teacher: Yes, we were. [Reading from a book] 'They may dress differently and speak differently but Africa is home to them all.' So where are we from?
Children: Africa

Another strategy I observed of both reinforcing a connection between people around the world and validating their own identities is the work that occurs of highlighting the physical beauty of those people and relating it to the beauty of the children themselves.

Mama Aaliyah: What do you notice about these people?
Cecilia: They're brown people.
Mama Aaliyah: They're brown people…
Michael: They're different.
Mama Aaliyah: Are they different but beautiful?
Children: Yea.
Mama Aaliyah: In fact, they're not that different because we just had our Kwanzaa play. Is this the kind of thing that we wore?
Children: Yes.
Mama Aaliyah: Are they beautiful?
Children: Yes.
Mama Aaliyah: They kind of remind me of you guys.
Cecilia: They're cutie pies.
Mama Aaliyah: They're cutie pies like you guys.

Mama Fela is a fan of saying that

> the establishment of identity and what's good about you starts really early and having a positive reflection of you, your people, of cultures that you can identify with in your home, in your neighborhood, with your family and how things happen with you, is useful.

Through this focus on identity, an effective global community allows regular opportunities for children to experience such validating reflections. As seen, there is real thought that goes into supporting children to develop a sense of personal power at the earliest possible point in their life at Little Sun People.

Lessons in Power

Figure 5.2 Children honor Marcus Garvey and other international Black and Brown heroes and activists

In the 1970s and 80s several schools existed that actively taught a curriculum which rejected the Euro-centric model that many early education programs adopt by default. Uhuru Sasa was one of these independent schools where "they were listening to all different people like Amiri Baraka, Herman Ferguson…" and others who taught the importance and value of locating oneself within the diaspora. Little Sun People is a clear descendant of these schools. The evidence can be found in the choice of international figures children learn about and the language used to describe them (see Figure 5.2).

After Swahili one afternoon, the conversation turned to Marcus Garvey and the choice to create a new flag that would unite Black people across the world.

Teacher: Girls, who brought us our first flag here?
Girls: [in unison] Marcus Mosiah Garvey.
Teacher: Marcus Mosiah Garvey. Why did he bring the flag here?
Children: Because we didn't have a flag for all Black people.

And another example appeared while exploring the queens of West Africa.

Global Citizenship Education in Practice: Little Sun People

Teacher: Who's this here?
Children: Yaa Asantewaa
Teacher: Who remembers the language that she spoke? Everybody say Twi.
Children: Twi.

Still another appeared when learning about Pedro Campos, leader of the Puerto Rican Independence Movement.

Teacher: Who's this man right here.
Children: [yelling different names].
Teacher: Baba...?
Children: Pedro...
Teacher: Pedro Campos. Where was he born?
Children: Puerto Rico
Teacher: What language did he speak.
Children: Spanish

Through these examples it is clear that there are two primary criteria for determining which figures are highlighted in the lessons.

1. That they are members of the diaspora.
2. That they actively resisted racism, colonialism and/or the spread of empire in their respective corners of the world.

It becomes apparent in these large and small ways that learning to be powerful (and utilizing the tool of validation by aligning their identities with others across the world who work to empower their communities) involves messaging to children that their responsibility is to be active participants working to make their world a better one. This participation in the strengthening of their home is part of what will make them active and engaged citizens in the world.

Affection and Care

Affection is another way that teachers at Little Sun People message to children that they have the power to positively influence their environment and the people around them. Sorrells (2012) quotes McIntosh, who noted that "within this vast world, the marks of a global citizen would

Lessons in Power

need to include affection, respect, care, curiosity and concern for the well-being of all living things" (p. 70). Expressions of affection and care are most apparent at Little Sun People in the informal conversations between teachers and children.

Worksheet 5.1 Opportunities to Practice Care in the Classroom

Affection: Am I communicating with children in ways that make them feel loved?

Respect: Do I listen to my children and respond directly to what they're saying? Do I trust my children?

Care: Am I modeling kindness? How do I comfort my children when they are feeling sad? Scared? Hurt?

Curiosity: Am I genuinely interested in what my children are interested in? How do I express this?

Concern: In what ways do I acknowledge the things that are important to my children? How am I responding to their feelings and their needs?

Mama Aaliyah can be characterized as an affectionate teacher. Her pet names for children make them smile. She expresses genuine interest in their stories. While talking one on one with a child, she makes eye contact and when interrupted, she comes back to the conversation with gentle encouragements: "keep going babe" and "I'm still listening. You have my attention". She expresses an eagerness to spend time with the children and at breakfast will often eat her meal with them. On a typical morning, the children, who have the option to bring their own breakfast or eat the provided hot breakfast, will share with her what they are having. On one particular morning in response to a child describing the egg in his breakfast, Mama Aaliyah said "I have eggs too. I'm going to go get my egg salad so we can have out breakfast together, ok? Have our protein". The combination of interest in and affection towards children teaches them that their

Global Citizenship Education in Practice: Little Sun People

Figure 5.3 Teachers intentionally build in opportunities throughout the day for children to talk about and practice care and affection

ideas and experiences are worthy of attention and that they themselves are worthy of love and affection. This, then, is a lesson in power in that it creates a world for children where their presence causes a reaction from others that messages to them that they are valued and provides a model for them to emulate with others.

> What are two simple ways that you can infuse affection and care into your children's day?

Hugging, high fiving, holding to comfort and being verbally affectionate towards children are regular practices in the classroom. In her article on teaching caring, Recchia (2008) cites Noddings, who describes a caring teacher as one who "not only responds to individual children in ways that make them feel cared for, but also in so doing, they model what it means to care for others for the whole group" (p. 70). This modeling is intentional. Gerhardt (2006) describes how affection actually assists in shaping the brain's capacity to interpret human emotion. Community engagement hinges, necessarily, on the capacity for emotional intelligence and the ability to discern what a person is feeling and needing. The teachers also encourage the practice of affection between children. This is from a conversation in early March 2014:

Lessons in Power

Teacher: What does embrace mean?… It's what we give our loved ones… they embrace to show their happiness and support. Can you give your friend an embrace?
[children hug and laugh].

It's important to note that although this feels like a game to the children, they are learning that in a healthy community, affection is something that is given and received freely (see Figure 5.3), in a variety of ways, and without hesitation.

Care is expressed in subtle ways in the classroom as well. On a Monday in May, three girls sat on the circle time rug. The first girl gripped a book that she did not want the other two to read or even hold. Listening to their conversation it became clear that it had been her favorite book at home and her mother had donated a copy to the class. She understood the book to be hers, rather than a copy, and the other two girls were attempting to convince her to share. One of the two immediately invoked the familiar "sharing is caring" in the attempt.

Nina: Benita gave this book to the class.
Cecelia: She doesn't want to share and that's not fun.
Benita: I don't want them to have it…
Nina: But sharing is caring.

Here the children exhibited an understanding of care not just as a means of leveraging control but as an action. At this point a teacher stepped in to reinforce a more dynamic concept of care for the group by reminding Benita that her mother read her the book at home because she cared about her and had given the book to the class because she cared for them as well. With some coaxing, the book was passed to the other children. The girls proceeded to "read" a few pages to each other before passing the book to the child next to them, practicing giving, offering and sharing something of value between them.

Care is also regularly modeled among adults for children. I observed many moments of tenderness between teachers in the presence of children during the school day that ranged from subtle accommodations to explicit articulation. The school is a busy place with numerous activities happening simultaneously and negotiating space is a challenge. Adults often have to adjust their plans for the day due to competing priorities.

On an unusually cold morning the weather forced everyone inside and with the back room occupied, half of the Asantewas (another classroom) had nowhere to do movement. After a moment of discussion together, the Fouriors teachers motioned to one of the Asantewa teachers. "Come over and have a dance-off with us." Putting her arm around her colleague's shoulder, Mama Aaliyah laughed. "You still got it, right?" The two laughed heartily. Behind them, one of the observing Fouriors children put her arm around her classmate's shoulder, mimicking her teacher's movements. The class, though crowded, proceeded to have a boisterous twenty-minute movement session, imitating each other to the sounds of Fela Kuti.

Agency

A direct source of power is the encouragement of children's agency within the classroom. Markstrom and Hallden (2008) have found that when children's perspectives are taken into account and they are acknowledged as competent decision makers, they begin to influence their classroom and environment in positive ways (Figure 5.4).

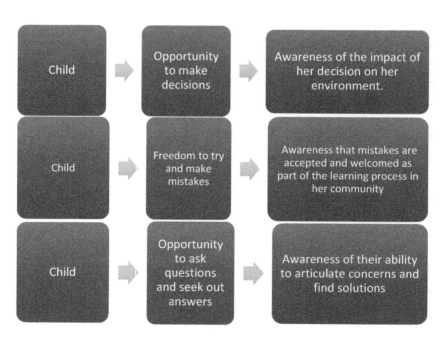

Figure 5.4 Agency's impact on children's contributions to the community

Once again, it begins with Mama Fela's taking control of her own daughter's education. With the decision of "I'm gonna start my own place. And I did", agency through self-determination became a theme of the school.

This theme shows up in the classroom commonly through regular conversation. During circle time a conversation developed between the teachers and the children about what to do in the event that they got lost. One teacher asked if everyone knew their mother's and father's numbers and followed up by explaining that "If you ever get separated, you tell a police officer your name and give that number". Questions followed about what to do if they couldn't find a police officer and the teacher reassured them that it didn't need to necessarily be a policeman and that any adult would do. Several children were noticeably relieved by this and began to practice sharing their numbers with each other. The knowledge that they had permission to interact with strangers in the event of an emergency combined with the comfort of having a strategy for doing so became a source of confidence.

Often in class, children are given control over what activities they choose. Each day at the morning meeting, children choose what activity they will go to during what is known as "center time". This agency gives the child a level of control over a portion of their day. In addition to this, the children decide on the direction of particular activities that teachers have chosen. On an art-heavy afternoon immediately after Swahili class in which the children had reviewed the names of animals, Mama Aaliyah turned the question of what to do over to the half of the class doing drawing. By asking "so which animals do you want to draw today?" and then following their direction, she gave control of the activity to the highly active group, effectively calming and focusing them. These moments and others like it succeed in giving children experience of being the decision makers in their world.

Lastly, the freedom to articulate needs and wants in negotiation is a form of agency that was constantly observed in my time at Little Sun People as the children navigated their space. Conversations around sharing occur regularly and bartering is a form of communication. Interactions often start with some form of "you can have one if I can have one". It's not clear how this negotiating came to be such a common way of communicating but the skill serves as a means of relating to one another and as a way of acquiring what one wants.

Self-Regulation

While power is learned through validation and agency, it is also learned through the development of mindfulness and self-regulation. Mama Barabi (see Figure 5.5) came to Little Sun People on Tuesday and Thursday afternoons to teach any child whose parents were interested in paying a small extra fee. Her yoga classes tended to have anywhere between twelve and eighteen children. Stretches were done by "making a yoga pizza", traditional poses such as shoulder stand were called "bicycle" and sun salutations involved barking like a dog and "wagging your doggie tail". In addition to the more active poses, called "waking up our energy", there was a strong emphasis on finding peace within oneself. Mama Barabi asked throughout the practice if each child felt calm, encouraged slow and deep breathing, and at the end of each practice brought out her singing bowl, a favorite of the children's. Each child who wanted to was welcomed to take a turn listening for the low hum of the bowl. All the while, Mama Barabi encouraged quietly. "Can you hear it…? You have to be calm and quiet and peaceful inside to hear it. That's your energy." It was a personal triumph when each child caught the sound of the bowl and, with the teacher's help, came to understand that it was their own inner quiet that allowed them to find the singing bowl's fading song.

Figure 5.5 Mama Barabi helps children practice mindfulness through yoga and meditation

Elsewhere in the classroom, self-regulation is practiced in other ways. The school is busy and noisy all day. The sounds from other classrooms are easily heard in the Fouriors room due to there being few floor-to-ceiling walls. Still, a certain point in most

> When during the day do children have the opportunity to slow down? How can you build moments of mindfulness into their day?

afternoons is designated for quiet play. With the low hum of activity in the background, children are encouraged to play or read quietly on the circle time rug. The level of concentration achieved is impressive to observe as children become completely absorbed in this process. Often a teacher is present to redirect a distracted child but for up to thirty minutes, three or four children are given the opportunity to lounge on the rug, absorbed in their work and oblivious to the noise around them.

Another example that illustrates the teachers' willingness to teach both self-regulation but also independence is chess teacher, Baba Norman's, strategy. Often, as children are sitting at the board, his coaching (see Figure 5.6) is steady and calm. "Show me something. Very good. Show me something else. What is that? Why did you move there…?"

Figure 5.6 Baba Norman guides a group of children through a series of chess maneuvers

Global Citizenship Education in Practice: Little Sun People

Worksheet 5.2 Lessons in Power

Goal	Questions to Explore	Collaborating Partners	Materials	Indicators of Success
Children feel heard and validated.				
Children recognize and provide affection and care within their community.				
Children display strong decision making and agency.				
Children are able to regulate their feelings and behavior.				

Without leading the child, he sits back to allow them to think about their next action and requires that they explain their movement. At times when a child is about to make a hasty move, he says, "Stop. Think about that". Often, the child will pause with a furrowed brow, head in hand, before making a different move. "Good" is the simple feedback. This practice effectively conditions the child to slow down and consider their decisions before acting.

As a result of the regular self-regulation practice, children are equipped to do things for themselves often. Within and across classes, it is assumed that children are capable of making decisions, carrying out jobs and following complex directions without help. For instance, when asking for help, a child is often met with "let's see if you can do it yourself. You guys are the big ones". In this way, teachers are always available yet trusting that children can act on their own and children learn through sustained practice that they are capable and able to influence their surroundings.

References

Gerhardt, S. (2006). *Why love matters: How affection shapes a baby's brain*. The Quality of Childhood Group, European Parliament (Presented in 2009).

Markstrom, A., & Hallden, G. (2008). Children's strategies for agency. *Children and Society*, *23*(2), 112–122.

Merriam-Webster. www.merriam-webster.com

Oxford English Dictionary. www.oxforddictionaries.com

Recchia, S. (2008). Teaching caring: Supporting social and emotional learning in an inclusive early childhood classroom. In C. Genishi & A. L. Goodwin (Eds.), *Diversities in early childhood education; Rethinking and doing* (pp. 67–82). Routledge.

Sorrells, K. (2012). *Intercultural communication: Globalization and social justice*. SAGE Publications.

Watts, R. (2013). *Power in family discourse*. Walter de Gruyter Publishers.

Little Sun People
Self-Esteem Development

In addition to lessons in power, an effective global citizenship classroom experience contains both literal and abstract opportunities to develop positive self-esteem. Healthy self-esteem development is defined here as the positive thoughts a person has of themselves and the high value that the person places on their life. Bergami and Baggozi (2010) list self-esteem as a primary characteristic of healthy identity development within a group. Generally speaking, self-esteem is reinforced by the ways that the child's community responds to their presence, identity and decision making. Running through all the categories described here is the concept of "belonging". Phinney (1996) speaks to the power of belonging when they assert that they "would expect that group identity, that is, a positive sense of belonging to one's group, would contribute to self-esteem" (p. 166). This chapter outlines how the community at Little Sun People reinforces this sense of belonging to strengthen each child's positive self-esteem development.

Identity

Although conducted with an older group of children, Phinney and Chavira (1992) outlined how self-esteem was directly related to identity. According to Mama Fela, the reason it is important to develop positive self-esteem early is because "there are so many people who are Black and Brown who are struggling because… there's a whole other side of them that has never been lifted up" in school, in their own community and in the wider world.

Self-Esteem Development

Little Sun People attempts to counterbalance this with a curriculum that highlights all of the ways that their children are important by celebrating their identities.

Mama Fela is very clear about her motivation to focus on positive identity development. "Our children need to take in that the truth about them is very positive. Their people and their cultures are wonderful." In order to achieve this, intentional lessons in children's self-worth begin as early as possible in the youngest classrooms at Little Sun People where children are as young as two years old. When events occur that reflect the painful reality of people of color in the United States, like the death of George Floyd in 2020 at the hands of the police, families are called in to process together with the teachers. Often at these meetings, parents ask for suggestions of how to talk to children about what's happening. The most commonly used strategy is to do what Mama Fela calls "loading in the positive" (see Figure 6.1). The loading often comes in the form of daily, preemptive conversations about "the greatness, the beauty and the miracle of who our children are, how amazing their families are and how wonderful their communities are".

Rather than offering conversations to children about painful subjects such as racism and death that they may not even be asking about, teachers lay a foundation about the fundamental goodness of the children and people who look like them across the world so that as they grow up and encounter images, perspectives and stereotypes that attempt to criminalize and devalue them and people who look like them, they are able to

Figure 6.1 Children are regularly told that they, their families and communities are fundamentally good as a way of laying a foundation of pride and confidence to challenge negative messages they may receive about themselves later on in life

75

Global Citizenship Education in Practice: Little Sun People

say "I know something different about myself" and remain firm in their understanding of who they are. It stands to reason that if they are fundamentally good and people who look like them are also fundamentally good, then abuse and racism that they face at the hands of others is wrong. "It lays the foundation for a sense of justice."

Showing children the "something else" of their identity early in order to encourage healthy self-esteem is done in a variety of ways at Little Sun People. As mentioned, the population at the preschool is predominantly Black and Brown and families, over the years, have come from nearly everywhere in the diaspora including the Caribbean, West and East Africa, Central and South America. Parents have expressed concern about the type of education their children would be receiving elsewhere. According to Mama Fela, "parents of those in what I call the global majority realize their children end up having to give up everything, their people, their cultures… everything that they've known, and totally accept a different framework". This does not have to be. The solution is also not to deny the European perspective entirely. As Mama Aaliyah explains, there is always balance (see Figure 6.2). "What we try to do is expose our children to the

Figure 6.2 The school provides materials and resources that reflect the cultural makeup of the children in the various classes

Self-Esteem Development

fact that there is an everybody else. We don't try to say that there isn't a European perspective… but in this little window, when you're here, meet these others."

As has been mentioned, numerous bodies of research have found correlations between a belief in one's personal physical beauty and healthy self-esteem (Patrick et al., 2004). Perhaps one of the most overt ways that identity reinforcement through positive self-esteem is taught at Little Sun People is by constantly telling the children that they are beautiful. Dolls, books, food, movies, artwork, community trips, music, the presence of Black and Brown teachers and daily conversations all corroborate to tell children that they are not just physically beautiful but also highly valued. This goes beyond the "food, music and holidays" form of multiculturalism that is present but impersonal in many schools and speaks to a culture at the school that daily and directly acknowledges the children at Little Sun People. By regularly drawing comparison to children in other parts of the world, this education acknowledges the unique and valued physical attributes of the children in the classroom while simultaneously educating them about the culture of others.

> How do you provide opportunities for children to explore their cultural identities? Do they feel integrated, consistent and daily or like add-ons to an already existing structure?

Teacher: [reading] African girls love to wear beads in their hair.
Cedella: [to her neighbor] Look at my hair. Mine has beads on it the same as you.
Teacher: That's right. [pointing to the picture] Her beads look a lot like yours. They're beautiful.
And later in the day, while looking at pictures in a book by herself on the rug…
Sue: [to herself] If you're brown… if you're brown, you're beautiful.

At the moment, Bedford-Stuyvesant is in a near-constant flux, with many older families of color who have lived in the neighborhood for three and four generations moving out and younger, wealthier, White families moving in. As a result, the community that many families who have children at Little Sun People have come to know and rely on as a source of safety is changing.

77

Global Citizenship Education in Practice: Little Sun People

> A lot of our African heritage community that typically live in and around Bed-Stuy, Crown Heights and other neighborhoods…are being moved out and so more and more White people are moving into the brownstone neighborhoods.
>
> (Mama Fela)

The changing demographic has caused a sense of anxiety around what this has the potential to do to the self-image of children in the community. This anxiety is transformed into positive energy with teachers more motivated than ever (Figure 6.3) to teach the concept of a unified community that sees its children, values their beauty in all of their forms and recognizes their gifts.

Self-Confidence

I became aware early on that the children in the Fouriors room regarded me curiously. I did not observe shyness when I was introduced as a guest in the classroom. The children immediately wanted to ask questions about who I was, how old I was, how long I'd be in the classroom and whether I had my own children. The confidence was joyful and unselfconscious and spoke to the safe space the children knew themselves to exist within at the school.

Luke: You ever been here before?
Me: Mm-hmm, I've been here before.
Luke: Nope. I never seen you. That's ok though. You can be here.

Within a month, several children were in the habit of asking me to join their play. Others enjoyed saying my name, trying out the device I used to record with and updating me about what had happened between my visits.

Cedella: Mama Robin [laughs]. Hi Mama Robin.
Sue: Oh, Mama Robin, can you play with the girls today?
Marie: Why do you hear it [pointing to my phone]?
Me: It's recording what you girls are saying.
Marie: What's this for? [pointing at the red bar moving on my screen]
Me: Whenever you talk, those bars go up and down.

Self-Esteem Development

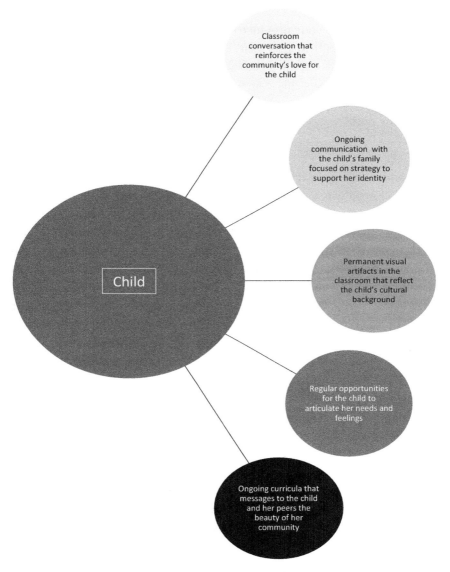

Figure 6.3 Consider all of the identities that each child brings into their classroom. How are those identities reflected in the curriculum, in your conversations together and in the physical space?

> Are children in your presence confident enough to use their voice to express their needs and feelings? Does this cause you anxiety or discomfort? Why or why not?

Communication and verbal expression are rarely discouraged in the classroom. Children are asked throughout their day about their opinions, asked to make decisions and encouraged to express how they feel about a variety of topics. During breakfast, as the children approached a long weekend, a little girl exclaimed with a sigh, "I need a break from school!". What followed was a conversation between the teacher and two or three children about why it was ok to feel tired sometimes at school and how even she (the teacher) needed a break sometimes. Her emphasis fell on how, even when she got tired, it did not mean that she did not love the children. Another time, I arrived late in the morning and sat down next to a child working with Legos at the table, who wondered, more to himself than to me, "Why would a big person sit next to me?" without hesitation or concern about my response. The following week one of the younger children in the class had a disagreement with a classmate who grabbed something out of his hand. Instead of retaliating, the younger child's small voice carried across the room, "I don't like that. Don't do that to me!" articulating clearly and comfortably both how he felt and the changed behavior that he expected from his classmate.

Mimicking adults appeared to be a major way that children developed their communication techniques and they often tried out various phrases overheard from adults in their conversations. This strategy increased their vocabulary and their capacity to express themselves with confidence. Being heard therefore became a powerful tool of self-confidence and enabled them to interact with peers as well as adults effectively. For instance, in the exchange below, the first child's rather unkind response to his friend's efforts at getting his attention are met with a commonly heard phrase from the adults in the building. The reference sparked a recognition of meaning in the first child and caused him to rethink his message and to reassure his classmates that their friendship was still intact.

Sue: Michael, I need that piece.
Michael: My ears are closed.
Sue: That's not nice. No secrets today. No secrets or surprises.

Self-Esteem Development

Jamie: Are you even our friend?
Michael: We're all friends. It's ok. We're all friends. It doesn't matter.

On another day, two children in the block area started arguing. On the other side of the wall a third child popped his head up from dramatic play and admonished the two, "don't even think about doing that", in a voice mimicking another teacher's gentle but firm style. At another time, during a conversation on healthy eating during lunch, one child offered for my approval: "One day I ate all my vegetables". I responded that I hoped today would be another day like that to which a second child, not originally a part of the conversation, piped in: "I want today to be a listening day". Apparently, my phrasing triggered a memory of something similar an adult said to or around him and he had found a place to insert it into our conversation.

The negotiations between children, strengthened by their increasing vocabularies and encouraged by an environment that supports their perspectives, is relevant here as well and contributes to children's positive self-esteem. The interaction documented below between two children in which they negotiated over the sharing of lunch is a perfect example of the influence of negotiating on the child's developing self-confidence.

Cedella: I want a turkey piece. Michael, can I have a turkey piece?
Michael: No.
Cedella: [face falls] Fine. Then you're not getting my [her voice trails off]...
Michael: [looks up surprised] Um, you can have the cheese.
Cedella: [firmly] No, I don't like cheese. I like turkey.
Michael: Here [hands her the turkey].
Cedella: Thank you.

The conversation is valuable in its entirety because it's important to note the range of emotions experienced between the two children. Cedella was initially extremely disappointed that her friend was not in the mood to share. She, however, had the presence of mind not only to inform him that he would not get what he wanted out of the situation if she did not get what she wanted, but to stand her ground when he offered her something less than satisfactory. She found that, by using her voice, she was able to get what she wanted out of the negotiation, which was a huge boost to her ego.

Global Citizenship Education in Practice: Little Sun People

Another way that the teachers work to intentionally build the children's self-confidence is by giving them multiple opportunities to be independent. Having assigned jobs each day allows the children to have both a sense of responsibility for their classroom as well as independence. The teachers assist them very little in their duties, from lifting and straightening the various small pieces of furniture throughout the room to bringing needed materials from room to room. This hands-off approach carries over into teacher-led activities as well. When helping the children understand new material, scaffolding is a useful tool wherein previously learned information is used to introduce new material. Often the teacher will lead the children to the information and leave it to them to discern its meaning in context.

Marie: I don't know how.
Teacher: Do you remember the piece that looked like this one that we used before?
Marie: Yes [looks around] hmm…
Teacher: Let's see if you can do it.

Baba Norman employs the same methods and his firm teaching style works well in these scenarios.

Baba Norman: Very good. Show me something else. What is that?
Luke: The rook.
Baba Norman: Why there?
Luke: Because it blocks the king.
Baba Norman: Good.

During a morning meeting in February, Nelson Mandela was quoted by a child practicing for the Black History Month celebration of his life:

> I learned that courage was not really the absence of fear… but the triumph over it.

The curriculum at Little Sun People incorporates an ongoing list of popular, successful and powerful people of color. This theme of personal greatness is just another example of the type of self-confidence messaging typically taught throughout the year. Children internalize these messages through their conversations with teachers about these figures, through extended periods where they engage in projects centering on their lives, through learning quotes and songs written by and about them and through multiple opportunities to reflect on their relationship to them in school and at home (families are encouraged to continue the conversations with children outside of school). The evidence from the Fouriors class is that children eventually begin to understand that the greatness that these adult figures possess is a natural element of who they are as well.

Community

When Mama Fela decided to keep her own children out of the local Brooklyn schools, it was because she feared for their emotional and psychological development as Black children in predominantly White schools where they were not going to learn that they were valued members of their local community or that they were members, equal to their classmates, of a much larger global community. As she puts it: "When I became a mom I said, 'oh my God, I have to stay home because I can't put them in these schools'". As her grandson finished his schooling at Little Sun People a few years back, she reflected that "I have a grandson now who is graduating from here. I would never encourage my daughter to put [him] in any of those schools".

There are multiple layers of community at Little Sun People. Pictures of the children and their families are visible in each classroom and effort is made to create a seamless bridge between the child's home life and their life at school.

Families play an integral part in creating the culture of the school and it's important that they feel at home. Knowing the struggle that Black and Brown families often face to feel welcomed and valued in schools, the teachers at Little Sun People work hard to create a community where families belong. Parents organize themselves into subcommittees. Some think about enrichment, others build fundraising opportunities, while still others focus on outreach and family engagement. A group is often responsible for

> When do children have opportunities to explore their communities? How are they and their families encouraged to see themselves as valued members of those communities?

Figure 6.4 Fathers serving during the Umoja Karamu, or Unity Feast

creating teacher appreciation days. Fathers and other male figures cook regularly for the Unity Feast, Umoja Karamu (see Figure 6.4). Everywhere families are validated. This speaks to the commonly heard mantra at the school that "what's good about you starts really early". The deeply entrenched presence of their families sends a message to each child that they and their families are wanted and welcomed in their school and creates a culture of extended family where all are working towards the shared goal of supporting children.

Another overt way that strong community is reinforced is through the practice of emotional intelligence. Mama Aaliyah has worked hard to set the foundation for an environment where both teachers and children know what their community members need and actively practice it. Part of effective engagement in community is the ability to read different

Self-Esteem Development

emotions to understand what appropriate response is needed. Many of the books read in the Fouriors classroom focus on interpreting emotions and responding effectively. *No, David* is a favorite book among the children. They've memorized it and become extremely animated when it is read.

Mama Aaliyah: [reading] I said No David!
Jamie: He's crying.
Mama Aaliyah: What else? Tell me another feeling.
Luke: Mad.
Sue: Embarrassed.
Mama Aaliyah: Embarrassed. Why might he feel embarrassed?
Sue: Because he's not listening to his mom.
Mama Aaliyah: That might be a reason to cry.

The children seem to enjoy identifying the various emotions. Having had practice, it is easier to know when a friend or peer is in need of the appropriate response.

Sue: You look upset. Want me to help you? Let me help you wipe the carpet.
There's no one to help you. I'll help you a tiny bit.

Knowing that they reside in an environment where their emotions are properly interpreted and where the right response is regularly offered assists in teaching the child that they are safe to articulate their needs and that those needs will be met. On the giving end, good global citizens (as defined by Gaudelli, 2003) who know how and when to respond to their fellow community members are being developed.

The children's connection to the neighborhood is a priority at the preschool and perhaps the most prominent evidence of intentional community building at Little Sun People. Building out from the family, the next concentric circle children exist in is defined by the relationship they have with the neighborhood that the school is located in and features prominently in how children's self-image is developed. The Fouriors walk through the neighborhood every day that the weather allows and have conversations about what they see. Sometimes these conversations are self-generated and at other times they are actively engaged in conversation around a theme by their teachers. At times, the conversations center on the physical aspects of the streets that they walk through.

Michael: The ground has cracks
Sue: That's concrete. The concrete is old. It has cracks.
Teacher: Why do you think that is?
Sue: It's because they haven't fixed it yet.
Dion: Our school isn't on this street. It's on the next street. I wish they'd fix this one and make it look nice.
Teacher: Why should they fix it?
Dion: They should be able to walk and not trip. We walk this way every day. We should be able to walk and not trip.

Here the children are encouraged to examine their physical surroundings in relation to themselves (see Figure 6.5) and name their expectations for their environment while also identifying a way that their community can care for them.

In this way, they begin to understand that it is their right and their responsibility to live in communities that honor and respect their needs.

Whether taking a walk through the neighborhood, witnessing their family's multiple forms of engagement within the community or properly identifying a need their peer has, children are daily learning the work of operating within community (Figure 6.6). This practice will benefit them once they leave school as they will be equipped with the tools necessary to be successful community builders and community members in the world. As Camicia and Saavedra (2009) name, these experiences ultimately

Figure 6.5 A class out for a morning walk in the neighborhood

Self-Esteem Development

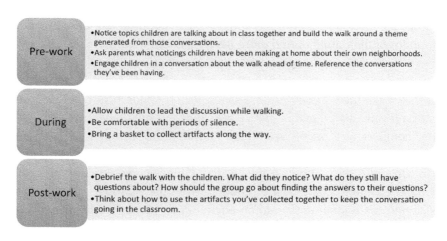

Figure 6.6 Taking a community walk

"promote the knowledge, skills and dispositions necessary for students to nourish democratic communities" (p. 505).

Little Sun People: Conclusion

Tension over the deaths of people in the African diaspora, the mass recording, reproduction and distribution of the images of these deaths and the subsequent rallying around them puts the question of who wields power (and how) even more prominently at the forefront of conversation in our society. Racially inspired brutality in the United States has been an ever-present nightmare for people of African descent since their arrival (Russell-Brown, 2006). The uniqueness of this particular moment in American history is that it is receiving more media attention than at any other point in a generation. As a result, children of color are more exposed to images of people who look like them facing brutality from authority figures. Power was defined in this section as "the messages children receive about their ability to be heard, acknowledged and responded to in ways that centralize their needs and experiences". Children are inundated with images which have the potential to teach them that their words, their communities and their very lives are not worthy of life (The Opportunity Agenda, 2011). This causes a slow shift of power where the child begins to understand that they are powerless in the world in which they live. This disempowerment in turn

Global Citizenship Education in Practice: Little Sun People

causes the child and soon-to-be adult to move about in fear of the world, doubtful of their abilities and more likely to attribute power to the people they witness abusing people who looked like them.

The curriculum at Little Sun People is both global and anti-colonial in that it counters these very messages. When children of color receive constant validation that their lives have value and simultaneously that they are members of a large, welcoming and affirming community, they are empowered to adopt a different identity. A particularly interesting way that this concept is driven home is the fact that Little Sun People's student body is almost entirely comprised of children from the diaspora. Visually this is stunning. Children enter into an environment where nearly every child (and every adult) looks like a member of their family and community.

Framing the child's community as global and the child as a central member within that community eliminates the concept of an assigned space that they are meant to occupy according to the images and messages they receive outside of school. The child is free to be compassionate, witty, caring, intelligent, shy, brave, extroverted and any other number of characteristics that best suit them. Simultaneously, understanding the world as their personal community as a result of an intentional structure at Little Sun People where their own families and neighborhoods are integral players within the global community they are presented with every day, they build their self-esteem practice to move freely about the world with a sense of ownership. "Place" becomes a concept that they learn is self-determined as opposed to assigned. In this way, the child is emancipated from the idea of living within a limited space. The work is done so that, one day, as adults, the children will live expansive lives, less hindered by the limitations society attempts to put on them.

In analyzing the experiences of children, there is the repeated trend of exposing the child to a series of circles of community (see Figure 6.7).

At any given moment, the child occupies a number of different communities: their immediate family and school community, their extended family and a global community. The curriculum at Little Sun People locates the child firmly and intentionally within all of these spheres daily, messaging to them that their position in the world is determined by their definition only.

When Mama Fela states that "our children need to take in that the truth about them is very positive", she is challenging the counter-messages of trans-historic educational colonialism which tells her children that they

88

Self-Esteem Development

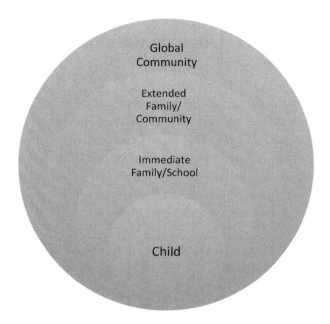

Figure 6.7 Global citizenship education at Little Sun People

are inherently bad. Healthy positive self-image development is central to emancipation from such messages. Mama Fela and the teachers at Little Sun People are actively doing the work of pushing back on power and privilege (Dei & Asgharzadeh, 2001) necessary for such anti-colonial work in the classroom.

When children engage in these practices at Little Sun People, they are learning a uniquely different story about themselves. Surrounded by teachers, immediate family and peers who validate them, children come to understand that living in a world that values them is normal. When they encounter people and situations that imply otherwise, they are then capable of internally recognizing both that 1) this is not their truth and 2) they have the tools to combat such inaccurate messages.

Little Sun People is a sanctuary, not free from the bumps and struggles of the community it represents, but constantly expanding and contracting in response to it. It is a place where children and teachers alike are actively engaged in the work of reconceptualizing what it means to be a member of both the local and the global community. It is a place where children can develop socio-emotional and cognitive skills while also learning how to operate as a complete member of a community made up of people who

Worksheet 6.1 Documentation: Self-Esteem

Documenting a particular theme in our classroom gives us the benefit of focusing on one element of the environment for a sustained period of time. This allows us to identify where rich global learning is happening and what resources and strategies children are using as well as where possibility exists for more learning to happen. This tool can be repurposed for any of the elements of global learning presented in this book.

Examples of Children Exploring Their Identity in the Classroom	Tools, Resources + Strategies Used	Date
Examples of children expressing self-confidence in the classroom		
Examples of children enacting community in the classroom		
Other examples of self-esteem in the classroom		

look like them who are generous, empowered, creative and in control of their lives and their community. While children at Little Sun People are building the idea of who they are individually and in relationship with their immediate community, they are simultaneously exploring their identities in relation to their extended community, the global majority. This vast community becomes a homeplace full of people who love, prioritize and value them.

References

Bergami, M., & Baggozi, R. (2010). Self-categorization, affective commitment and group self-esteem as distinct aspects of social identity in the organization. *British Journal of Social Psychology, 39*(4), 555–575.

Camicia, S., & Saavedra, C. (2009). A new childhood social studies curriculum for a new generation of citizenship. *International Journal of Children's Rights, 17*(3), 501–517.

Dei, G., & Asgharzadeh, A. (2001). The power of social theory: The anti-colonial discursive framework. *The Journal of Educational Thought, 35*(3), 297–323.

Gaudelli, W. (2003). *World class: Teaching and learning in global times.* Lawrence Erlbaum Associates.

Patrick, H., Neighbors, C., & Knee, C. (2004). Appearance-related social comparisons: The role of contingent self-esteem and self-perceptions of attractiveness. *Personality and Social Psychology Bulletin, 30*(4), 501–514.

Phinney, J. (1996). Ethnic and American identity as predictors of self-esteem among African American, Latino and White adolescents. *Journal of Youth and Adolescence, 26*(2), 165–185.

Phinney, J., & Chavira, V. (1992). Ethnic identity and self-esteem: An exploratory longitudinal study. *Journal of Adolescence, 15*(3), 271–281.

Russell-Brown, K. (2006). *Protecting our own: Race, crime and African Americans.* Rowman and Littlefield.

The Opportunity Agenda. (2011). www.theopportunityagenda.org

PART

Global Citizenship Education in Practice
Mid-Pacific Institute

Mid-Pacific Institute
The Context of Community

The original inhabitants of Hawai'i were highly skilled maritime navigators who arrived from across Polynesia around the 2nd century, CE. Bringing with them an exhaustive knowledge of farming and fishing, the residents understood that their relationship to the land was not simply symbolic. The Kumulipo, commonly understood among Hawaiians as the story of their creation, is a history of life on earth but it is also

> a genealogical prayer chant linking the royal family to which it belonged not only to the primary gods belonging to the whole people and worshiped in common with allied Polynesian groups… but to the stars in the heavens and the plants and animals useful to life on earth…
>
> (Beckwith, 1951, p. 8)

The relationship between humans, the earth and the universe itself is one of lineage and this philosophy influences all aspects of Hawaiian culture. As one would care for a mother or father who provides us with all that we need, so too is it the responsibility of humans to nourish, sustain and protect the land. The renowned sovereignty rights activist and historian Haunani-Kay Trask (1999) explained that "since the land was an ancestor, no living thing could be foreign… Nature was not objectified but personified, resulting in an extraordinary respect for the life of the sea, the heavens and the earth" (p. 5). Following this model, it is a misalignment to understand our positionality as consumers without also identifying as replenishers and conservators of the world we live in.

DOI: 10.4324/9781003005186-11

Within this cosmology, a society arranged itself around a series of Aliʻi (high chiefs), who were endowed with the responsibility to provide for and keep order among the communities of the newly discovered islands. Families were free to move from Aliʻi to Aliʻi and no land could be bought or sold but was instead passed through lineage. The reign of ʻUmi-a-Līloa is often referenced as an example of the powerful and effective Aliʻi who ruled the islands. ʻUmi-a-Līloa is known as being the first chief to unite the government of Hawaiʻi, bringing stability and prosperity to the nation. As a result of his good works, political prowess and reputation as a caregiver to the common people, he is known as a common ancestor to the people of Hawaiʻi.

Within this structure, an economy developed which was built on the responsible use of resources and based on the Kapu, which guided all aspects of community life. Islands were divided into ʻokana, which were further and further divided into tracts of land that ran from the mountains and fanned out towards the sea. This land was then used in cooperative ways by extended families, or ʻOhana, to grow crops such as taro, bread-fruit and starchy bananas and to raise pigs and chickens, among other animals, which their ancestors brought with them from their homes in the South Pacific. In this way, a society based on mutual respect and collective responsibility for the land on which it depended was built.

Seventeen years after Cook's arrival, the Kingdom of Hawaiʻi was established by Kamehameha the Great in 1795, who had himself come from a long line of powerful Aliʻi. Unification of the islands occurred under Kamehameha in 1810. America's first exposure to the islands in the 1820s brought traders and missionaries to the islands and Hawaiʻi's convenient location in the Pacific as a point of trade meant that it became hotly contested land. The Tyler Doctrine in 1842 indicated to European powers that the islands were, essentially, unavailable for use as they were economically valuable to United States' interests; a mentality of foreign ownership (without proper compensation) descended, informing the United States' relations with the nation for the next fifty years. A review of literature on western perspectives on Hawaiʻi points to a profoundly racist attitude towards the inhabitants of the islands and a general consensus that the land was better off under the control of wealthy American landowners who could better manage the islands for their own economic gain. The US Committee on Foreign Affairs considered it the country's right to utilize

The Context of Community

the tiny nation's resources and encouraged Americans to think strategically about how they might benefit from this use.

As early as 1859, US planters were advocating for Hawai'i's annexation. Kamehameha III, though originally resolute in his resistance against the imposition, allowed the Reciprocity Treaty of 1875, which granted the United States access to the nation's fertile lands on which the country soon made a massive fortune in sugar. This moment is a source of great pain among many Native Hawaiians as it signaled the eventual loss of the islands' independence some years later through forced annexation to the United States in 1898.

Lydia Lili'u Loloku Walania Kamaka'eha, or Lili'uokalani (see Figure 7.1), Hawai'i's last sovereign and only queen, is known both for her generous treatment of visitors and skilled diplomacy as well as for her devotion to her people and enduring effort to first keep and then win back

Figure 7.1 Her majesty, Queen Lili'uokalani, last regent and only queen of the sovereign nation of Hawai'i

the sovereignty of the nation. The Queen's presentation of a new constitution, accompanied by the support of two thirds of the nation's population, was seen as a direct challenge to the business interests of American Sanford B. Dole, eventual president of the Republic of Hawai'i, and other powerful landowners. These men had begun to make their wealth off of the nation's vast plantations and a new constitution favoring the rights of the Hawaiian people threatened their economic interests. The Committee of Safety, a group whose purpose was to assist in the annexation of Hawai'i to the United States, began an effort to overthrow the kingdom in 1893. After an attempted coup in response by Hawaiian royalists, the Queen was sentenced to imprisonment within the confines of her own home in 1895.

In her autobiography, written while imprisoned in the upstairs quarters at Iolani Palace, the Queen's usually fluid and solicitous tone gives way to pain and, at times, fury as she reflects on the signing of the Bayonet Constitution in 1887:

> ...having matured their plans in secret, the men of foreign birth rose one day en masse... and forced the king, to sign a constitution of their own preparation, a document which deprived the sovereign of all power... and meant that from that day, the 'missionary party' took the law into its own hands.
>
> (p. 80)

With very little constitutional power available to her, the Queen found herself cornered. Although her majesty petitioned multiple US presidents, Hawai'i was annexed in 1898 and a new government was set up with Dole serving as president.

Due, in part, to the need for labor, the new government serving the increasing population of landowners solicited help from numerous Pacific-bordered countries including Japan, China and Korea. Missionary communities also ballooned during this time. The period is known for its exceptional rate of immigration and trade, which would ultimately lead to the islands becoming one of the most diverse states in the country, a status it maintains to this day. It would also further displace and disempower a large number of Native Hawaiians on their own land who were subjected to their native language being banned and their culture suppressed. Still, a fervent renaissance of Hawaiian culture and activism exists today with many continuing to advocate for Hawai'i as sovereign land, never willingly given to the United States government.

Early Education in Hawai'i and the Creation of Mid-Pacific Institute

King Kamehameha III established the first public school system in Hawai'i in 1840. Since then, the commitment to early education in Hawai'i has grown into a full-fledged state-wide initiative to educate all children between birth and eight years old through the Hawai'i P-3 program and an active Head Start and Early Head Start program. The state utilizes research-based evidence to inform its understanding of the benefits of Pre-kindergarten and its investments in programs such as Parents and Children Together which works to actively engage parents and communities in whole child care, including mental health and wellness and economic opportunity for the state's most vulnerable populations. The numbers vary, but by estimates, there are more than eighty private preschools, as many as four hundred and thirty-seven public preschool options and nearly eight hundred and thirty licensed family childcare providers across the state.

In 1864, Kawaiaha'o Seminary was incorporated to educate Hawaiian young women with the intention of training them in biblical study, deportment and hygiene and home skills such as baking, home maintenance and needlework. Notably, academics were intentionally left out of the curriculum (Pratt, 1957). A second school, Mills Institute, was created in 1892 for the education of Chinese boys with a strong focus on civic duty and responsibility to the laws of the United States. A third missionary school, Okamura Boys Home, served Japanese boys starting in 1896. A fourth, the Korean Methodist Mission, was created as an outgrowth of Mills to serve Korean boys in occupied space adjacent to Mills.

Although serving undeniably different goals (Kawaiaha'o's mission to train young Hawaiian women in the home arts clashed with the academic and international relations agenda of the other three schools), all four had in common the orientation towards what was defined at Mills as the concept of a "conscientious service to community". Okamura eventually merged its upper grades with Mills, making the population at Mills a combination of Chinese, Japanese and Korean young men. In 1905, Mid-Pacific Institute was formed by the joining of Mills and Kawaiaha'o Seminary under the motivation of creating strong diplomatic relationships between the cultures of the Pacific-bordered countries.

Figure 7.2 Kawaiahaʻo Hall on the unified Mid-Pacific Institute's campus

Philosophical divisions remained for some time after the merger, mainly because the vision of a school that promoted international understanding and peace education (Hussey, 2014) could not reconcile with an agenda that limited the education of its Hawaiian young women to homemaking skills. Similarly, across the various schools, there remained the desire to Christianize students, which at times discouraged their varied and culturally meaningful traditions in favor of more Americanized ways of knowing. Even in the midst of these tensions, we begin to see the development of a globally oriented curriculum inspired by authentic engagement with community. Westcott (1923) identifies within student learning experiences at the time a "devotion to social duties; that which directs us to joys which grow greater as they are shared…". It also becomes apparent that the cultural experience at the school provided meaningful social value among the Asian students in attendance. In her article, "Growing up Asian in America", Goodwin (2003) reflects on this experience among Asian American students in mixed race school settings where they have access to one another. "Being able to see oneself reflected in the faces of others, as well as not being the only 'Other' but one among many 'Others' seems critical to understanding the various ways in which [students] constructed their images of self" (p. 10).

Mid-Pacific Grammar and High School was established in 1923 (see Figure 7.2). In the following decade, the nearby Epiphany School, an outgrowth of the Episcopal Church, welcomed its first class of kindergarten-aged children and rapidly expanded to include the elementary grades.

By the 1980s, Epiphany had adopted a more progressive and constructivist approach and ultimately severed its ties with the church to merge with Mid-Pacific. The result was a preschool through high school program (see

The Context of Community

Figure 7.3 High schoolers at Mid-Pacific in the 1950s

Figure 7.3 for an image of a midcentury high school class) that was especially diverse, even by Hawai'i's standards, with an orientation towards Christian education and the influence of Hawaiian philosophy threaded throughout.

Mid-Pacific Preschool and the Reggio Emilia Approach

The town of Reggio Emilia (see Figure 7.4) sits in the Northern Central region of Italy at roughly the midway point between Florence and Milan. It is recognized as having an effective, responsive government and an active, cooperative community oriented towards organizing across ethnicity and class lines who are socially engaged and encouraged to advocate for themselves and others.

Pre-primary schools (dedicated to children between three and six years of age) are an integral part of Italian culture, having arisen first through private charitable contributions and moving towards the public sector in the first half of the 20th century. Educators like Bruno Ciari and Loris Malaguzzi believed that children's early education environments should liberate them, recognize their rights as full members of society and respond to the continual social changes happening around them.

For Malaguzzi, the school's physical environment was an active additional teacher in this pursuit. It is a living thing that takes on multiple forms in its relationship to the child. At times, it is a place where friendships are

101

Figure 7.4 The town of Reggio Emilia

built and sustained. At other times, it is a place for arousing curiosity and experimenting; a place where multiple ideas and perspectives are invited in. An intentional democracy. At still others, it is a sanctuary where the child could see their own work and their own process all around them.

Multiple educators work in concert with the classroom to provide this environment for the child. Among them are a pedagogista who is primarily concerned with supporting the teachers in observing, listening to, documenting and helping to identify themes and ideas that are developing in the child's world. Also present in the classroom is an atelierista, whose role is to maintain an art studio stocked with a wide variety of materials for children to manipulate and discover a variety of their own skills. Their role is also to assist teachers in understanding how children make meaning of their world through this process of manipulation and discovery.

Head teachers and teachers are co-learners and community members alongside children. They may bristle when asked what they "teach" and may prefer to say that they facilitate learning instead. They are listeners and documenters and are responsible for curating learning spaces that encourage the child's voice to be elevated as their natural development occurs, independently and in concert with one another. Malaguzzi understood that in order to be an empowered member of a community, a child must first have the experience of understanding that they are both the creators and sustainers of their world (Edwards et al., 2012). The development of this agency and confidence in their ability contributes to the child's understanding of themselves as active and valued members of their community.

In the Reggio classroom, the natural world is integrated into the life of the school and children are encouraged to expand their learning

The Context of Community

beyond their classroom through trips into the environments surrounding the school. Intentional explorations and meaning-making of what they encounter together as a group are encouraged and new ways of seeing and understanding the world are championed. hooks (1994) understands that "children make the best theorists… Since they do not yet grasp our social practices as inevitable, they do not see why we might not do things differently" (p.5 9). As most early developmental theorists understand, they are scientists by nature and when their ideas are welcomed and reflected back to them by the adults around them, their identities as seen and heard members of their community are strengthened.

The Early Learning Centers in Reggio Emilia are structured in this way. Malaguzzi named that "among the goals of our approach is to reinforce each child's sense of identity… so much so that each one would feel enough sense of belonging and self-confidence to participate in the activities of the school" (Edwards et al., 2012, p. 45). Belonging and self-confidence are developed when the child's environment makes room for the many ways that they theorize about their world. Malaguzzi's poem, "No Way. The Hundred is There" demonstrates why this is so important.

The child
is made of one hundred.
The child has
a hundred languages
a hundred hands
a hundred thoughts
a hundred ways of thinking
of playing, of speaking.
A hundred always a hundred
ways of listening
of marveling, of loving
a hundred joys
for singing and understanding
a hundred worlds
to discover
a hundred worlds
to invent
a hundred worlds
to dream
The child has

a hundred languages
(and a hundred hundred hundred more)
but they steel ninety-nine.
The school and the culture
separate the head from the body.
They tell the child:
to think without hands
to do without head
to listen and not to speak
to understand without joy
to love and to marvel
only at Easter and Christmas.
They tell the child:
to discover the world already there
and of the hundred
they steal ninety-nine.
They tell the child:
that work and play
reality and fantasy
science and imagination
sky and earth
reason and dream
are things
that do not belong together.
And thus they tell the child
that the hundred is not there.
The child says:
No way. The hundred is there.

> ("No Way. The Hundred is There" by Loris Malaguzzi, translated
> by Lella Gandini © Preschools and Infant-toddler
> Centers – Istituzione of the Municipality of Reggio Emilia)

The freedom to engage in this identity work is valuable and helps to define what it means, in the case of the town and schools in Reggio Emilia, to be Italian as well as what it means to be a global citizen.

While still at the Epiphany School, a group of educators along with their director, Dr. Edna Hussey, visited Reggio Emilia to observe their schools in action and returned "fully alive". They succeeded in convincing their governing board that if they could open an early learning center affiliated with Mid-Pacific, it should be a Reggio Emilia inspired program.

The Context of Community

The merger of the Epiphany School into the structure of Mid-Pacific Institute occurred in 2002 and the preschool was established in 2004. Although the structure of the curriculum at the institute at that point had been an inquiry-based philosophy, it was inquiry that originated primarily from the adults. When the preschool began to engage in work that was Reggio influenced, it shifted the way the rest of the school approached inquiry-based work. Learning became child led.

Today, the preschool is located adjacent to the elementary school on Mid-Pacific's sprawling forty-three-acre campus in the picturesque Mānoa Valley of Oahu (see Figure 7.5). The individual classrooms have been combined into one mixed-aged classroom based on teachers' observations of what children were needing. The atelier in the Reggio Emilia tradition serves as a unique experiential space in which to create and to utilize all the senses in a developing relationship with the world. Ateliers are usually stocked with a wide variety of natural and man-made materials of various textures, colors and sizes. The more effective ateliers provide access, at least in part, to stores of materials indigenous to the community the child inhabits; familiar things with which to understand the world they live in and directly influence through their manipulations. The atelier

Figure 7.5 Mid-Pacific Institute's elementary and preschool campus

Figure 7.6 The atelier at the preschool

at Mid-Pacific (see Figure 7.6) is a feast for the eyes, containing an ever-evolving blend of materials, found, new and up-cycled, for children to access and manipulate.

Six teachers, including the head teacher, pedagogista and atelierista, support thirty-two three- and four-year-old children in a warm, flowing classroom that reflects the variety of cultures represented in the Valley. Spaces are curated for collaboration and exploratory play while corners are carved out with lamplight, cozy seating and even an upright piano, to reflect the familiar and the safe.

A typical day in the three- and four-year-old room begins with arrival between 7:45 am and 8:20 am. This is a time for parents to do a drop-off that is broad enough to honor the children's various morning routines. It's also a social time and children are welcome to engage in free play. An open group meeting typically happens at 9:00 am, which is usually based on a project the children have been working on or a question that's come up. Sometimes, the meeting is twenty minutes and sometimes children engage each other in conversation for an hour. The teachers in the room work to not stifle these conversations and adjust the day accordingly. After snack, children work indoors or out, depending on the idea they're exploring. It's encouraged that if they have been inside, they then spend time outdoors in what the teachers refer to as the outside classroom. Lunch generally occurs at noon and children rest or nap afterwards. If children are picked up after nap, a family member is encouraged to wake their children up, creating a cycle to the day that begins and ends with the families' presence within the school. The afternoons are for quiet time and the remaining children stay in afterschool care, which tends to be less structured.

The Context of Community

I first encountered Mid-Pacific Institute during the presentation of "The Wonder of Learning: The Hundred Languages of Children" exhibit at the University of Hawai'i and its accompanying conference on Mid-Pacific's campus in 2013. Our days were spent observing a seemingly endless display of art, curiosity and meaning-making in the Reggio tradition through the exhibit, exploring the preschool classroom and atelier space and learning together with Mid-Pacific's preschool team as well as Reggio Emilia inspired teachers from across the country and the world. When we were not in session or visiting classrooms and exhibits, some of us headed to the beach while others trekked into the hills and spent the day among the trees (Figure 7.7). Using various materials, we followed the path the children themselves had taken to make sense of who the wind

Figure 7.7 A sketch of the trees and vegetation from the author's trip into the hills surround Mānoa Valley with other Reggio Emilia inspired teachers

Reflection

Who are the original inhabitants of the land where you live? Are they still a part of the cultural makeup of the community? Why or why not?

Are there ways that the schools in your community support healthy relationships between the different cultural groups who live there?

Are there cultural traditions that exist within your school that are not represented by the student body? What purpose do they serve?

What is your school's schedule? Is it determined by the needs of the families it serves? The needs of the teachers? The community? Something else? Why or why not?

was and where it went on the island. We began to build a relationship with it, following along as it was visiting Oahu's various cultural landmarks and identifying itself with the island and its people. These experiences deepened my understanding of what it meant to support child-centered learning and have stayed with me these nine years.

Mid-Pacific is engaged in an active conversation about its student body and the ethics of its identity as an exclusive school in a state as culturally and economically diverse as Hawai'i. The year I reconnected with the preschool there were seven children whose families identified as Japanese, Chinese or Korean, one child who was White (American), one who was White (French), four children who were of native Hawaiian descent and thirteen children whose families identified as having mixed ancestry. Both the pedagosita and atelierista are originally from Ohio and moved to Hawai'i, while the lead teacher and director of the preschool were born and raised in Hawai'i.

References

Beckwith, M. (1951). *The Kumulipo: A Hawaiian creation chant – a history of the mythology, folklore and gods of Polynesia.* Pantianos Classics.

Edwards, C., Gandini, L., & Forman, G. (Eds.) (2012). *The hundred languages of children: The Reggio Emilia experience in transformation.* Praeger.

Goodwin, A. L. (2003). Growing up Asian in America: A search for self. In C. Park, A. L. Goodwin, & S. Lee (Eds.), *Asian American identities, families, and schooling* (pp. 3–25). Information Age.

hooks, b. (1994). *Teaching to transgress: Education as the practice of freedom.* Routledge.

Hussey, E. (2014). *Learning the other: The evolving identity of a merged school.* University of Hawai'i at Mānoa.

Lili'uokalani, Queen of Hawai'i. (1898) *Hawai'i's story by Hawai'i's queen, Lili'uokalani.* Lee and Shepherd.

Luke, A. (2009). On indigenous education. *Teaching Education, 20*(1), 1–5.

Malaguzzi, L. et al. (1996). *The Hundred Languages of Children*, exhibition catalogue, Reggio Children, Reggio Emilia. www.reggiochildren.it

Pratt, H. G. (1957). *The story of Mid-Pacific Institute*. Tongg.

Trask, H. (1999). *From a native daughter: Colonialism and sovereignty in Hawai'i*. University of Hawai'i Press.

Westcott, B. (1923). As quoted in *The Friend*. April (p. 86).

Mid-Pacific Institute
Membership in Community

In his text "Teaching for social justice, diversity and citizenship in a global world", Banks (2004) describes global citizenship as occupancy within a community that establishes a fine balance between a sense of unity with those of other communities and a firm understanding of one's own unique value. This global community acknowledges the individual student's perspective and values as much as it recognizes the cultures and perspectives outside of the student's own. At Mid-Pacific preschool, children are led through the creation of a "new thing", a hybrid of their individual, highly valued identities and who they become as a community when those identities encounter one another. If global citizenship is, as Meyers (2010) says, inspired by the goal of resolving global problems at the local level, the preschool classroom at Mid-Pacific is a laboratory for practicing the work of being in community with one another in preparation for the world beyond. Through their relationships, their collaborative effort and their elevation of traditional ways of knowing and interacting with the world, children are daily building the muscle of taking part in a global community.

Relationships

According to Leslie Gleim, pedagogista for the preschool, it makes sense that Reggio Emilia is the model for Mid-Pacific's preschool. In a community where respect for each other and the world around them is deeply rooted in who they are and how they treat each other, the Reggio philosophy reinforces the importance of relationships by complementing a value

DOI: 10.4324/9781003005186-12

system rooted in a community already deeply engrained in Hawaiian culture. This shows up in a multitude of ways at the preschool. Relationships ground the work of the teachers early in the school year as they engage in home visits to observe children in their most familiar environment and begin to understand how culture is honored in the home. The visits also allow children to meet their new teachers in the environment where they feel safest, which helps to remove a layer of the unknown for children before the school year starts. Respect is modeled to both child and family when teachers acknowledge and express interest in their child's safest of spaces.

In addition to home visits, families are invited to share who they are and to bring the home life of the child into the classroom early. Families send in photos and photo journals (see Figure 8.1) that they create, which tell the story of who they are and which are kept in the classroom year round.

Robynne Migita, lead teacher in the preschool classroom, shared that these artifacts are traces of the families that children utilize all year long to discover the similar experiences they have with their peers. Throughout the school day, the journals are readily available and children tell their family story to their peers. The journals and photos are also a comforting reminder of the familiar to children in a new environment or in a classroom with new faces, all of which supports their developing relationships with their peers. The teachers have found that encouraging families to share

Figure 8.1 Photo journals created by families are kept in the classroom year round

Membership in Community

meaningful bits of home with the classroom also supports the relationships between teachers and families. "Parents want to know we love and respect and see your child from the beginning. That has to be there among the teachers and the school. Then they are open to listen and to trust."

The teachers are intentional about both curating creative opportunities for current children to learn from one another and honoring an ever-evolving space that reflects the community of children who have passed through the classroom. Originally, the threes and fours occupied separate spaces but when

> What are the important elements of a healthy relationship? How have the teachers in your life modeled healthy relationships? How can you model healthy relationships for your children?

the teaching team observed the rapid socio-emotional and cognitive development and synergy that occurred when the ages were put together, they decided it made more sense to keep the children in the same environment; the classroom has been blended in this way since 2013. In addition to creating a space where mixed ages benefit from their interaction with each other, the current year's children are regularly exposed to the communities of children from past years who have moved through the space that they currently occupy. In many classroom environments, teachers strip the room at the end of every year and re-build it according to a new group of children who enter in the fall. The teachers at Mid-Pacific choose not to strip the classroom but continually add to it as new children enter the space (see Figure 8.2) so that prior years' children are as much a part of the community as the current class. This messages both to older children who have moved to ongoing schooling as well as to younger children currently occupying the classroom that they are a part of the 'Ohana of the preschool.

Regardless of their own background, Dr. Hussey hopes that through relationships, "children will absorb and learn to accept and be open to different cultures and perspectives". Problem-identifying and solving together is a part of this process. Areas of the indoor and outdoor classroom space are carved out for this kind of inquiry work and the priority of making inquiry student- rather than teacher led lends itself well to explorations where children are in charge of identifying questions and finding the answers. "We're not there teaching, like it's a hierarchy", Jordan Hasley, the atelierista, explains. Robynne builds on this: "We're creating

Global Citizenship Education in Practice: Mid-Pacific Institute

Figure 8.2 Documentation, created by the teachers, showing several years' worth of children's explorations

space for the children to explore how they feel about a certain topic and take the lead on finding a resolution". What inevitably happens when children lead is the moment "when they turn to each other and recognize each other's strengths in their community and start seeking each other out. That's another turning point in the year".

Relationship across the entire community, including the natural and man-made world, is a priority at Mid-Pacific (see Figure 8.3). Asking themselves "how do children come to know who they are in the world?", the teaching team relies on the rich tradition of storytelling, acknowledging that "Hawai'i's history and creation are steeped in cultural legends and stories about the islands. The stories of the island have been handed down and told from one generation to another". The tradition of storytelling has become a primary way for the children to connect to their home, yard, neighborhood and, eventually, the world around them. The classroom learns legends every year, often facilitated by Kumu such as Kumu Moses, an indigenous Hawaiian storyteller, actor, playwright and member of the community. Through him, children are encouraged to absorb and re-tell

Membership in Community

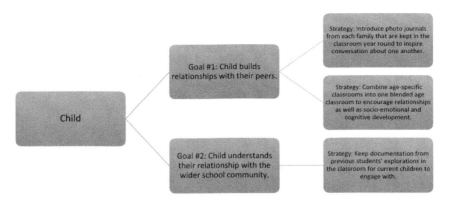

Figure 8.3 Creating an environment conducive to building relationships

the stories in ways that make sense to them. There is a level of empathy and connection that they make as they re-tell and internalize the stories and over time become storytellers themselves, relating to and making sense of the world through them.

For instance, in 2019, the children engaged in an exploration of what a Mystery was with the teachers identifying themselves as co-constructors in this inquiry. Utilizing various "research sites" such as the school grounds, the local Target store and the island of Oahu itself, children assigned anthropomorphic thoughts and emotions to each place to explore what caused a mystery to be a mystery in each location but also, what each place might be feeling and thinking. By interpreting their surroundings in this way, children began to develop relationships with each place, leaning deeply into the understanding, created long before they came to be and illustrated as early as the Kumulipo, that we are in direct relationship with the world around us.

Another example of this relationship-building process with the world around them was the experience teachers guided children through when the government proposed building a new high-powered telescope on Maunakea, a dormant volcano and sacred site on the island of Hawai'i. The move created a deeply contentious struggle between Native Hawaiians and the government as the construction represents the desecration of the home of the ancient gods of the nation to Hawaiians. Massive protests across the islands brought media coverage to the issue and children began to ask questions based on the conversations they were hearing all around them. To support their understanding, the teachers encouraged children to see the issue from the perspective of both the mountain and the telescope.

Figure 8.4 Children discussing Maunakea

They posed a guiding question: "What if someone came to your door and said 'We're taking your house'. How would you feel?"

By the end of the exploration (see Figure 8.4.) the, children had come to see Maunakea as a friend, with feelings, who they were in relationship with. They made sense of the conflict by naming that the mountain was sad at the prospect of the telescope being built on it because that was not its purpose. Afterwards, one child's family took him to Maunakea because he expressed the desire to see it for himself. When they returned to Oahu, the parent wrote the teachers saying that the child told them that Maunakea didn't want any more telescopes. Considering others in their community, both human and otherwise, with the same regard and thoughtfulness that they would want for themselves helped to facilitate a relationship with Maunakea based in mutual respect and drew them closer to understanding its needs and their fellow Hawaiians' protection of it. By seeing the mountain as a friend and exploring how they would feel in its position, the children related to it as they would a member of their community, which made it natural to want to care for it and ensure its well-being.

Relationships with the natural world around them has also led to strengthened relationships with schools and children across the world. While exploring the wind, teachers documented children's relationship building with the element online, attracting the attention of several international schools. One, in South Africa, reached out and a meeting between the two teaching teams was organized. The children had the opportunity to talk to each other, ask questions and share stories. Identifying with similar values, the school in South Africa eventually adapted the project to their own community of children and one of their teachers traveled to visit Hawai'i, meet with the teachers and share skills with the Mid-Pacific community.

As with any relationship, there are challenges. Dr. Hussey is transparent about the struggle it has been to reconcile Mid-Pacific's status as an exclusive private school with its mission of creating compassionate global citizens in relationship with the wider community. The school is expensive by Hawai'i's economic standard, which means that there are families who cannot afford the tuition. Hussey says it is "something I think about all the time; the messages that are conveyed to our children" about their relationships with others in other schools and other communities across the state. She notes that the ways that children under the care of the teaching team are learning about the lives of others is a weighted responsibility that the educators are constantly navigating.

The culture of the place assists with this. Robynne explains that "growing up in Hawai'i, we were raised to show gratitude to everyone who came before us because somewhere along the line, someone made a sacrifice for us". The teachers remind the children of this often by encouraging appreciation when someone assists them, supports them or cheers them on. The Reggio curriculum also assists with this. Leslie is a fan of invoking the Italian saying, "I am who we are", and engagement with one another at the school is dependent and personal. The message regularly imparted to children, she says, is that "It's not just me. We have to work for all of us". In this way, relationships are built from the perspective that, with each connection, the community is strengthened. Throughout the day teachers work to nurture these relationships, knowing that they are often the first exposure that children have outside of their immediate families. "We are first contact, and then the city and then the state, the country and the world and we realize this is the first step".

Collaboration

The value of collaboration is in the bones of Mid-Pacific. Well before the various schools coalesced into its current form, the early history of the school records that a portion of its land was set up as a dairy farm to help feed the children and the children themselves took part in its running. Older children produced all the pews for one of the large churches downtown and have maintained a collaborative relationship with the community ever since. The various schools placed emphasis not on the type of education that "concentrates our efforts on what we can gain for ourselves" but the kind which facilitates the sharing of gifts with one another (Westcott, 1923). Here the Italian "I am who we are" takes depth and identity is informed by how the community supports one another as well as how that sharing improves the world around them.

In the preschool, learning happens together. Group meeting time is held in a circle because it is a metaphor for the kind of collaboration teachers hope children will engage in; "It's corner-less". The team often references the children's perspective here and during planning time by telling them "we want to hear more about what you think about this". Curriculum building is also a way that teachers model meaningful collaboration and reflect children's perspectives back to them. The team is very intentional about not telling students what to learn but instead work to listen for the children to tell them what they want to know and incorporate it into the structure of the day. The teachers are aware of the impact this has on student learning. "How empowering is it to know that the teacher is listening so closely that you hear your own words back and through documentation, you see your work displayed prominently!" When a child has an idea, the group as a whole will try it out and find a solution together. In this way children become participants in the story of their school day, week and year (see Figure 8.5) and learn that they have agency in the creation of the kind of community they want to live in.

There is an authenticity that happens within the classroom when the student group that collaborates together changes from year to year. With each year, some children leave and some are present from the previous year. Each autumn, new children with new ideas and new backgrounds arrive and are welcomed into the collaborative work. Each time, the tone and perspective changes slightly, adding a new layer to the identity of the classroom. Children are exposed to new ways of thinking and problem solving and the "new thing" evolves as the various cultures and worldviews represented in the school come together again and again to create something unique and changing each year.

When asked when collaboration happens during the day, the teachers respond unanimously that it happens continuously. In the block area. In the

Membership in Community

Figure 8.5 Children collaborate all day long and teachers encourage them to find solutions to their problems together

outdoor play area. During meeting time. Children offer ideas and negotiate at a low hum throughout the day. The teachers' role is to create a space where children feel safe to experiment, to wrestle with ideas outside of their own and to find common ground. This skill is crucial as children and as adults in order to navigate a world of varying perspectives successfully.

There are many instances of this throughout the year. For the Mystery project, the children wrote a story together that they acted out with Kumu Moses. In small groups, they made mini murals of the parts of the story they'd been working on, which required collaboration and figuring out how to put their different graphic ideas together. For instance, one group wanted to represent a group of children listening to the story in their mural ("Do we use a round shape?"). Together, they had to come to a resolution. Through their practice they were able to land on a decision that accommodated everyone's ideas. Likewise, in a project called the Fantastical Project, children transformed a park they had been visiting into a magical landscape. Groups were formed with lots of back and forth designing of what would go into the park and how it would be created. The same type of negotiation and planning was practiced; two children struggled together over the design for a disco for the crabs in the park. Others imagined play opportunities and meaningful experiences for other inhabitants of the park. Through it all, the teachers witness, document and are present to provide support but work to not intervene as much as possible.

Leslie notes that when difficult things happen, "we don't run from them". The nature of Reggio inspired work is to welcome challenges as opportunities. For instance, if children aren't having conversations as a community about a difficult thing, the question among the teachers becomes "why not?" Why does the classroom not feel safe enough to have those discussions? What have children learned about themselves and their environment that makes this a challenge to talk about? Work is then done to collaboratively examine what can be done to make space for the topic.

It's also difficult sometimes when children make things, naturally take pride in what they've made and desire ownership of it. Conflicts arise and oftentimes teachers will hear "it's mine". To correct for this, efforts are made to use materials that are in abundance and can be replenished as often as possible. Natural and found materials are perfect for this in Oahu and the atelier features a rotating supply of materials indigenous to the island.

> What does collaboration look like in your classroom? What impact has the collaborative practice had on your children's confidence?

The preschool-aged child is regularly looking for cues for how to negotiate relationships. Being in an environment where healthy communication, empathy, collaboration and implementation of ideas as a group happens helps to message to children how they too are capable of healthy interactions that honor a variety of viewpoints. For instance, the children are always watching how their teachers communicate and collaborate with their families. What they see regularly are two parties who are mutually invested, from the beginning of the year, in being united on working through challenges together.

The teachers hope that children will be kind people who find happiness in sharing their gifts with others. This reflects the goals of the school's early administrators and illuminates the trust that adults have in their children's ability to navigate the world effectively. They have not been disappointed. Consistently, children show that they are capable of resolving conflict and participating in their community through regular collaboration. Built into their teachers' trust is also the hope that children never lose the joy

Membership in Community

of wondering about their world together. It is reminiscent of Malaguzzi's vision of spaces for children to express all of their languages in their explorations...

"The child has...
a hundred joys...
a hundred worlds to discover...
a hundred worlds to invent...

Hawai'i's Cultural Heritage

As we've seen, healthy global citizenship can be described as having the ability to do two things simultaneously. Global citizens have a deep love for and commitment towards their own home and community, that which they are born into or that which has been adopted. At the same time, they understand that they are part of a global community that is made up of many different communities, voices and stories, some of which are familiar and some which are very different. Hawai'i is an excellent example of how these many voices live together, not without conflict, but regularly striving for respect and appreciation. For instance, the massive tourism market across the islands has succeeded, over the years, in commercializing large swaths of traditional Hawaiian culture while often removing the original meaning and value behind what are often sacred actions (Trask, 1999). There is a need for greater respect for indigenous ways of being. This conversation across the state happens in fits and starts but, imperfect as it has been, it continues.

At Mid-Pacific, a parallel conversation is happening. Great effort is made for children to have space to develop their voice and identities through exposure to the many traditions present in Hawaiian culture which are taught by those whose communities practice them or by Mid-Pacific teachers with consultation with those in the community. Teachers are intentional about growing children's ideas about their positionality in

> How does the presence of multiple cultural perspectives in your program contribute to children's understanding of their position in the community? In the world?

121

connection to the world around them. They begin this work by honoring who the children are and who their families are in the ways named earlier in this chapter. When these families and cultures come together, an environment based on shared values begins to be created as children share, try out and explore, and take pleasure in each other's traditions and ideas.

Many people in Hawai'i identify as multi-ethnic as a result of the many communities who, over the years, have made Hawai'i home. This is reflected, somewhat, in the preschool's population. Dr. Hussey notes this when she reflects that "all of us are immigrants from somewhere. Even those who are Native Hawaiians brought their culture and traditions from somewhere". To assist children in navigating this multitude of perspectives, teachers have developed a strategy of utilizing some of Hawai'i's most valued traditions (while not excluding others) to instill respect towards the ways of living for all.

At Mid-Pacific this is evident in large and small ways. Adults call each other "auntie" and "uncle", an influence that comes from Hawai'i's tradition of utilizing the concept of a large extended family, 'Ohana. Children are also taught to deeply value the land and a garden is currently being planned by the children with plants indigenous to Hawaii that the children themselves will care for.

Yet another beautiful example of the way cultural heritage is acknowledged is the honoring of the elderly in the life of the school. Several cultures in Hawai'i emphasize respect for elders, or Elemakule, and there is a strong sense of love and respect for them in both the Asian and native Hawaiian cultures represented in the preschool. In addition to the open-door policy that welcomes families into the life of the classroom day to day, Grandparent's Day is a tradition that has existed at Mid-Pacific for twenty-five years. Typically, Kupuna are welcomed in to do an activity and spend time with their grandchildren and peers (see Figure 8.6). This type of reverence is not limited to one day as children are able to see and reflect on their elder family members' presence through documentation which stays up in the school for an extended period of time and inspires ongoing conversation throughout the year.

Exposing children to the narratives of the former nation's history is another way that the cultural heritage of the place, even those parts that are difficult, are addressed (see Figure 8.7). The atelierista, Jordan, talks about the moment the team brought the children into the city for the 120th anniversary of the overthrow of Queen Lili'uokalani as an example of bringing

Membership in Community

Figure 8.6 A grandparent writes a letter to her granddaughter while visiting the classroom for Grandparent's Day

children into contact with history. During the event, there was a large procession and the children were given cameras to document the day as well as to help them look back and reflect on what they were seeing and feeling in the moment. The intention was to continue the work of embedding the value of building relationships with the places and people (and history) that still impact the lives of Hawaiians today.

In preparing for this and other projects that face Hawai'i's history, Dr. Hussey explains that one thing they keep in mind is that the school population has a very small percentage of children who are native Hawaiian. At the preschool and elementary school level, the number is close to 5% of the population. Even still, when the team was preparing for the project, they did not avoid the topic of sovereignty simply because it was something that could be described as an adult subject but, instead, took the children straight into it.

As mentioned, storytelling is an important Hawaiian tradition that permeates every aspect of the school. Teachers think deeply about how to utilize this oldest of traditions and have both Kumu in-house who are storytellers as well as Kumu who live and work outside of the school

Global Citizenship Education in Practice: Mid-Pacific Institute

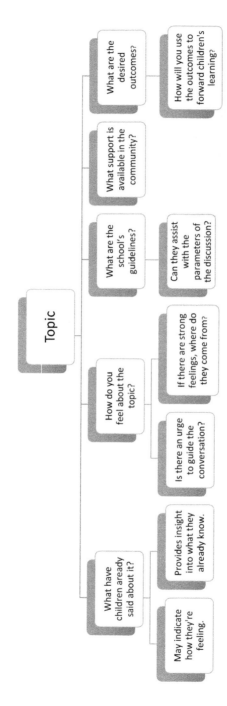

Figure 8.7 Supporting children's learning about cultural topics that are emotionally challenging

Membership in Community

Figure 8.8 Kumu Moses works alongside the teaching team to guide children through the proper ways of acknowledging and appreciating the land they live on

community and are skilled in teaching in modes that honor indigenous tradition (see Figure 8.8). This makes for a community of teachers who share stories with children on a variety of topics and in a variety of ways.

When it comes to learning about the cultural heritage of the place they all inhabit, Jordan explains that, through practice, the children come to understand that this place is their home and these traditions are ones that they have a responsibility to honor and respect. This is a direct pushback to what Wane (2008) describes as colonial history's efforts to de-emphasize indigenous knowledges and ways of being as primitive and less valued. When messaging the islands' history to children, it is less about teaching and more about living, by example, the ways of honoring the home they all share and how best to coexist together so that children learn to carry the richness of these ways of knowing with them. As Robynne says, "Everything is built on respect".

Global Citizenship Education in Practice: Mid-Pacific Institute

Worksheet 8.1 What/Why/How

Moving from a goal to a plan of action can be a daunting task. Breaking the work down into steps is an effective way to incorporate the goal into the life of our classrooms. This tool can be repurposed for any of the elements of global learning presented in this book.

Guiding Question

What does a child's integration into a vibrant and healthy community look like?

What do we know?

Why does it matter?

How do we support it in the classroom environment?

References

Banks, J. A. (2004). Teaching for social justice, diversity and citizenship in a global world. *The Educational Forum, 68*(4), 296–305.

Genishi, C., & Dyson, A. (2009). *Children, language and literacy: Diverse learners in diverse times.* Teachers College Press.

Meyers, J. (2010). 'To benefit the world by whatever means possible': Adolescents' constructed meanings for global citizenship. *British Educational Research Journal, 36*(3), 483–502.

Trask, H. (1999). *From a native daughter: Colonialism and sovereignty in Hawai'i.* University of Hawai'i Press.

Wane, N. (2008). Mapping the field of indigenous knowledges in anti-colonial discourse: A transformative journey in education. *Race Ethnicity and Education, 11*(2), 183–197.

Westcott, B. (1923). As quoted in *The Friend.* April (p. 86).

Mid-Pacific Institute
Stewardship

A simple way to think about stewardship is as the responsibility of taking care of something. Stewardship for the communities we live in and for the land that we live on is a part of the responsibility that members of a global community carry. At Mid-Pacific, the preschool is infused with the practice of caring for the world they live in. Children own this work in the ways that they make sense of their relationship to one another and their physical surroundings and their teachers create space for them to think, ask questions and experiment with ideas for how to do this. The focus on inquiry-based work allows for children to conceptualize solutions to the problems they encounter in their world and the freedom to enact strategies that make their world a better place. The student-led quality of this type of engagement ensures, as Malaguzzi envisioned, a space where "always and everywhere, children take an active role in the construction and acquisition of learning and understanding" (Edwards et al., 2012, p. 44).

Agency Revisited

The Oxford English Dictionary (2021) defines agency as "an action or intervention, especially such as to produce a particular effect". As we saw in the overview of development, young children learn, through interactions with the world around them, that their actions produce results. A toddler encountering a shallow bowl of water may splash the water's surface and discover a startling but ultimately enjoyable result. A preschooler may approach a pile of rocks, consider its properties and choose to build a car/garden/house/etc. Upon completing the task, I have witnessed many a four-year-old builder standing back and admiring their creation with pride. Research on the benefit of providing children with opportunities to practice agency tell us that early experiences of being given choice and control increase the child's confidence and, as was seen in the development chapter, their innate understanding of their ability to impact their surroundings when it is wanted or needed. Learning this lesson early is an extraordinary asset to the global citizen. Children grow into adults who understand that they have the power to experiment with their surroundings to create necessary change.

Mid-Pacific's inquiry approach evolved through the 80s and 90s. Originally, early education practice at Epiphany consisted of a lock-step approach in which teachers gathered to think about what they wanted children to learn and posed questions to children that the children were then expected to find the answer to. In this way, inquiry originated from the teachers. When the preschool was added to Mid-Pacific's structure, it changed the way the entire school thought about inquiry. Administrators watched how Jordan, Leslie and Robynne interacted with children, making space for their voices and honoring their interests. It became obvious that the student-led space was one where children were far more invested in their own learning.

Children's encounters with their peers and preschool teachers are often the first chance many of them have to establish independence and the adults work to ensure that in all of their interactions, they are nurturing that independence as well as children's awareness of their ability to advocate for themselves. In many more "traditional" adult/child relationships, children are not only directed by adults but encouraged to follow without a great deal of input or opinion. At Mid-Pacific, space is made for children to explore their perspectives on a variety of topics, to articulate them and are encouraged to have conversations with adults about them. They have the right to speak and share their ideas. They have the right to an opinion and to make decisions about their space. This practice, alongside one that embeds a deep valuing of the cultural heritage that surrounds them, assists children in developing a relationship within an environment where they are respected and with an environment they are expected to respect.

The practice of providing children with opportunities to practice agency is enacted in a number of small ways. From the beginning of the year, parents are encouraged to let children be responsible for and carry their own belongings in in the morning. "We tell them from the start that they can carry their own lunches", Leslie explains. As in all schools, children get bumps and bruises. They fall on their own and in the presence of others. Sometimes, if they get hurt, a child will look around, expecting the adult to intervene and make it better. Regularly, teachers will wait to see what the child does and many times, they are able to collect themselves and return to their activity. Over time, they begin to understand that they are capable and don't need to always turn to an adult to solve their problems (although the adult is always close by, ensuring a secure base).

However, there is more here. Jordan explains "we are letting them know that we know they can do it". It's not simply that children are learning that they are capable of overcoming challenges on their own. They are also learning and internalizing their membership in a community that has faith in their ability. The space to practice agency, independence and success in a curated environment under conditions where community members believe in their success creates a cycle where children are growing ever stronger and more capable of making decisions based on an understanding of their own innate competence.

When this happens, children gain confidence which they begin to utilize even when circumstances tell them there is no space for their voice or their presence. At one point in the year, the children visited a stretch of beach and witnessed bulldozers moving sand in large quantities (see Figure 9.1). When they returned from their trip, the children's conversations, as well as the teachers' documentation, informed parents

Figure 9.1 When children noticed a grandmother and her grandchild at a beach while it was being excavated, they took it upon themselves to write to the mayor requesting signage to make the beach safer

Stewardship

that their children were intrigued by the experience. A parent, who is also an oceanographer, was invited to visit and take part in the conversation about the topic and during their conversation with the children informed them that it was not safe to go into the water while the excavation was occurring. The children, however, had seen a grandmother and her grand-child near the water, very close to where the excavating was happening. Together the class began to talk about what they could do to make the beach safer for their neighbors. They determined that the best way to take action would be to alert the mayor and formally request that the city put up signage at the beach. Together with the teachers, they decided to create a proposal and the teachers brought in an expert to help them draft it.

After creating the document and while preparing to visit the mayor's office, a child mused that "maybe the adults should take [the proposal] because they're not going to listen to us small people". Here was evidence that the children perceived the mayor's office, and the people in charge of decision making there, as not being particularly interested in the viewpoints of preschoolers. However, because the children exist in a space where, daily, they are experiencing independence and agency and are surrounded by adults who listen to and trust them, they decided that it would be them that took the proposal to the mayor. They did encounter adults who condescended to them, just as they had anticipated, and yet they succeeded in their mission of voicing their concerns about the safety of their community members and pushed past their doubts because they had already come to understand themselves as members of a community that values their voice (Figure 9.2).

Similarly, when the children visited town on the memorial of the Queen's removal as the sovereign ruler of the Kingdom of Hawai'i (see Figure 9.3), the teachers were not concerned about their being overwhelmed by the crowd or by the content of the day. Dr. Hussey explains that the teachers trusted the children would be able to engage with the content. They had already had the experience of being in crowds, traveling around the island and navigating a variety of spaces and the teachers had confidence in their ability to be in such an environment without becoming anxious or overwhelmed.

The children were capable and succeeded in moving about the space without teachers needing to coddle or worry. They also were not told how to feel about the history the event highlighted but, rather, were encouraged to make their own observations and ask their own questions.

Global Citizenship Education in Practice: Mid-Pacific Institute

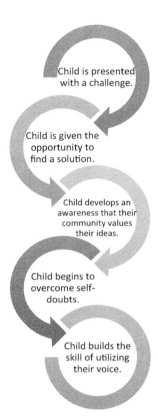

Figure 9.2 The impact of agency

This is not to say that they were left alone to make sense of such large concepts; instead, it was an opportunity for teachers to "listen sensitively to what the child was questioning and respond directly rather than trying to answer a question they were not asking". The developmentally responsive approach allowed time and space for children to absorb new ideas in ways that made sense to them and were more personalized to their comprehension.

During my time with the preschool team I heard the phrase "the curriculum belongs to the children" on four separate occasions. Children ask for and then hear stories so often because their teachers are constantly taking cues from and responding to their interests. It is also an exceptionally effective learning tool that has produced profound results. One preschooler in the class was quieter than the others. When legends were being told, she didn't say anything and never spoke up when children engaged

Stewardship

Figure 9.3 The class surrounding Queen Liliʻuokalani's statue during the 125th anniversary of her deposition

in conversations afterwards. It was clear that she was taking in the information however, because at the end of the telling, she would draw everything that she had heard. Her mom later recalled that, at home, her daughter was telling her every legend in the city that she had learned. Her ability to receive information in a chosen format followed by the freedom to absorb and interpret it in the ways she was most comfortable with produced an exceptional expression of her own voice.

Children come to believe that there is no limit to what they can do. They are safe to trip and fall and know that they are capable of getting back up. They know that they are heard and empowered to use their voice to accomplish goals. They develop preferences and chosen ways of learning and interpreting the world that are taken seriously and implemented often by the adults in their life. They take risks and in the midst of these expressions of choice, they know that they will be ok. These lessons become the foundation for the actions global citizens take to be empowered stewards of their world.

Responsibility to the Land and Ownership

Mid-Pacific's mission statement outlines the school's desire to produce "compassionate and responsible lifelong learners and global citizens". Both the Reggio Emilia philosophy and the influence of Hawai'i's commitment to stewardship support this task. At the heart of the work, the preschool community is driven by a sense of empathy for each other but also for the land. Empathy is not simply expressed as a feeling, however, but is enacted through a sense of responsibility to be advocates for the physical world. Italians speak of the "youngest citizens in the world" and Reggio educators understand the environment to be a supportive co-teacher in this work. Creating opportunities for children to practice what it means to be stewards of their home is intuitive and can be found everywhere in the work at Mid-Pacific.

One of the first elements of an identity as a steward of the land is in the recognition of how to respectfully enter meaningful spaces. One of the reasons teachers are so fond of working with teachers like Kumu Moses is because they regularly remind children that it is not appropriate to enter a space without acknowledging and offering gratitude to it for all that it provides to our lives. Sometimes Kumu Moses will offer a chant to pay respect and often will lead the children in giving thanks before entering and partaking in what the space has to offer. This reminder is helpful in remembering to pause to say thank you and recognize how our lives are better because of it.

> We live on an island and the land is sacred and limited. I don't know if I've ever encountered such great respect for the land as I have since I came to Hawai'i. That informs the work we do and what we want to pass on to children.

It is hard not to be inspired to give thanks when you are on Oahu. The Mānoa Valley, where Mid-Pacific is located, is majestic and lush (see Figure 9.4). At various times of the day, the fog rests on top of the trees in the rolling hills, and after the rain it burns off to reveal what looks like a never-ending rolling concert of green sparkling in the sun. Rainbows appear each day. The result of a still active volcanic chain, Hawai'i is being formed in real time and the rich soil plays host to a massively diverse ecological world. The ocean that surrounds the children's home has been a source of

134

Stewardship

Figure 9.4 Mānoa Valley

sustenance and spiritual connection for islanders, of which the ancient art of surfing is only one manifestation. In addition to being the pedagogista, Leslie is also an aerial photographer. Reflecting on the images of the land she captures from above, you begin to see how connected all of the islands are and how interwoven its communities are. Teachers are motivated to instill this appreciation and respect for the land in their children.

This appreciation is practiced in a variety of other ways as well. A conversation among the teachers illustrates best how the interconnected moments of acknowledgment and appreciation lend themselves well to embedding a sense of responsibility to the land in their children on a daily basis.

Edna: There's a strong belief in our stewardship of the 'aina in what we do. In what we grow.
Jordan: We spend so much of our time outside. It's just a part of who we are. The children are watering plants. Collecting little treasures…
Edna: There's a spirit and a soul in the land. The water. The air. The winds. Each of those elements have many legends here.
Leslie: And it's all filled with the mana. When we enter a new space, we enter with respect because we want the children to understand it's not just a space to have fun but a place to honor and preserve for the future.
Edna: Even the little things. You're not supposed to throw your lei in the trashcan. I always take it out and hang it on one of the bushes to return it to nature.

For Robynne, instilling a sense of responsibility is foundational and complements the act of carrying for others well. "It really comes back to valuing place and space because those lessons translate to how we want to treat people and the communities we live in." Children learn gradually how to care for the school and then for the natural world around them, much like how they came to understand their relationship with Maunakea. The various elements of the environment are teachers but are also community members alongside the children in this process. In expressing their care for their environment, the children are able to practice the work of being responsive to their community's needs. Seeing their role as being responsible for the well-being of world around them and engaging in relationship with the elements with empathy translates neatly into how they care for one another. The practice is a priority for the same reason that passing down legends to children is important; they will eventually be the caretakers of their culture and their home and therefore it is important for them to have the tools and knowledge to care both for the land and for one another well.

Once children are able to understand their roles as stewards of the land, and have developed the ability to transfer this understanding to their responsibility to each other, they are prepared to think of the whole of Hawai'i as a community that they are a member of and have a responsibility towards. At Mid-Pacific a great deal of thought goes into how to communicate to children that Hawai'i is "their Hawai'i". In fact, several years ago teachers began a project called "Our Hawai'i", which had a dual purpose. Through exposure to the meaningful places and traditions of the islands, children gained a greater appreciation for their home. Simultaneously, they were encouraged to look back at the history of the islands as a guide for looking forward and thinking about their own futures and responsibilities as members of the community (see Figure 9.5).

In the same way that children "own" the curriculum through their regular active participation in its evolution, so too do they "own" the responsibility of caring for the whole of the natural world that they live within. Whether through their being guided in a ritual of thanksgiving on sacred land, an exploration of how to use their voices to make their home a better, safer place or a sense of joy at their accomplishment (the "we did it" moments are particularly joyful for both the children and their teachers), children are learning early in life what it looks and feels like to carry on the tradition of stewardship.

Mid-Pacific Institute: Conclusion

The United Nations defines sustainability as actions that "meet the needs of the present without compromising the ability of future generations to

Stewardship

Figure 9.5 Children documenting during the "Our Hawai'i" project

meet their own needs" (www.un.org/sustainabledevelopment). This practice, like any other life skill, is most effective when it is learned early in life. In this way, our relationship to the world around us and each other becomes a vital part of our daily activity, not just an occasional responsibility. True to Malaguzzi's vision, at Mid-Pacific children come to understand that they are both creators and sustainers of their world and that both require their effort together as a community.

The culture of the preschool points to a gradual transformation from a "Me"-centered way of interacting with the world to a more sustainable "Us" orientation. As seen in the earlier development section, it is quite normal for preschool-aged children to enter their first formal classrooms with this "me" orientation. The educators in the classroom seem to be deeply aware of this cognitive and socio-emotional stage and work to blend developmentally responsive opportunities with expectations and values that are reflective of the community around them. The relational structure that is the result of this work is a perfect example of the distinction made at the beginning of the book between traditional multicultural education and more effective models of global citizenship education. As opposed to a framework that positions the child in the center of the world but disconnected from other people and communities who are positioned

Worksheet 9.1 Creating Stewardship Opportunities for and with Children

What opportunities do children have to be stewards in their classroom, in their community and for the land around them? How much input do they have in the decisions that are made about caring for their surroundings? Fill with a new set of opportunities monthly.

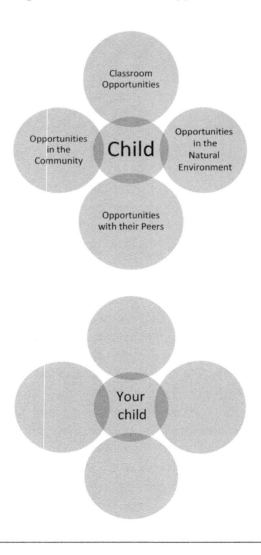

Stewardship

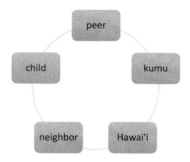

Figure 9.6 Global citizenship education at Mid-Pacific preschool

as beneficial to their lives but not quite equal in value, the global framework at Mid-Pacific places the child on an equal footing with those around them (their peers, educators, the surrounding community and the land itself) and in collaboration with them (see Figure 9.6).

Each thing, from the relationship-building opportunities that encourage respect for each other and the communities around them to the collaborative work that happens at every point in the school day, allows children to practice creating a kind of world that is more capable of sustaining itself over time and more aligned with the ways of engagement and knowing that the community around them have identified with for centuries. It is a practice that simultaneously allows children to look back by referencing tradition and forward through the enactment of community.

This enactment is supported by educators who see their children as equally valuable and craft environments for them to practice engagement in a two-fold way. According to Jordan:

> Children get a sense of their position because we value them so much that we encourage them to have conversations with adults. It looks like them having the right to speak and share their ideas. The right to an opinion and to make decisions about their space.

In this environment, children first become familiar with their own voice and are empowered to use it towards the building of a world that reflects their needs and identities.

Simultaneously, children in this type of environment begin to seek out the perspectives of others who are learning to use their voices at the same time. As Robynne noted, there is a point in every school year when "[children] turn to each other" because they have begun to understand that they exist in relationships with peers who also make valuable contributions to their world. This searching out for each other's presence and ideas indicates that children are becoming aware that they exist in a world with identities and perspectives outside of their own that are equally valuable to their world.

This two-fold process directly reflects McIntosh's definition of global citizenship. Children develop an awareness and appreciation for their own identity and voice while also recognizing and valuing the multiple perspectives that make up the larger community that they live within. Children growing up in Hawai'i today are exposed to many different cultures and ways of thinking. The Reggio curriculum combined with the community's cultural ways of knowing intentionally enacted in the classroom environment make room for these various perspectives to coexist.

The teaching team lights up when they think of the impact of this work. "All of these little bits [of the children's identities] are like a tapestry woven together" by the way the team interacts with children, through their use of the classroom as an additional teacher and by the children's own motivations and creativity. In asking the teaching team what the ultimate goal is, they pause. "We want them to become advocates. We're constantly thinking about how to help them become a voice for good." This engagement is global citizenship in action.

As the former Mayor of Reggio Emilia, Graziano Delrio, states, "the child is a competent citizen" (Edwards et al., 2012, p. 83). When children have opportunities to collaborate, and be in relationship with one another, when they engage in their shared history and culture and when they experiment with what it looks like to be responsible for their home, they come to understand that citizenship is something deeper than a feeling. Rather, "[t]hey discover how satisfying it is to exchange ideas and thereby transform their environment" (Edwards et al., 2012, p. 67). At Mid-Pacific, that experience is made possible by the creation of a learning space where children are heard and responded to. The result is a place where children can practice their roles as stewards, imbued with a deep sense of respect for and obligation to their home.

References

Edwards, C., Gandini, L., & Forman, G. (Eds.) (2012). *The hundred languages of children: The Reggio Emilia experience in transformation.* Praeger.

Oxford English Dictionary. (2021). www.oed.com

The United Nations. www.un.org/sustainabledevelopment/development-agenda

PART

IV

The Work of Teachers

Self-Reflection

10

The teachers at Little Sun People and at Mid-Pacific Institute are from very different parts of the world and prioritize some ways of learning for their children that might be unrecognizable in each other's classrooms. Among the things that teams have in common, however, one significant practice that is woven throughout the day and year is the amount of time spent reflecting on who they are individually and collectively as a teaching team. Another is the connection that they make in understanding how this reflective process impacts their practice and their environments. In both teaching teams, the educators reach back to examine their cultural, geographical and philosophical influences and identities and actively draw them into their work with children. What helps to facilitate this, in both schools, are environments which allow teachers to bring their whole selves to their work and actively encourage them to articulate these identities in concrete ways for the betterment of the learning environments that they are building.

As has been shown, children learn to be global citizens by examining several identities: first the self, then how the self is located in the local and the global community. The educators at both schools follow a similar process as they experience their roles as facilitators, guides and co-learners with their students. In our final conversations, teachers reflected on what their own identity work looked like and how it impacted their relationships with one another as well as their work of supporting their children's identities as citizens of the world.

At Little Sun People, the teachers' ethnic and cultural backgrounds reflect the backgrounds of the families that walk through their doors every

DOI: 10.4324/9781003005186-15

> Is your cultural identity intentionally built into the life of the school? If so, how does it contribute to your teaching practice? If not, why not?

morning. The teachers all come from families with roots in various corners of the African diaspora and nearly all share, within their blood lines, a story of migration. One teacher, whose parents are from Barbados, was born in London and later moved to the United States. Another was born in the Dominican Republic and now makes New York City home. Two are deeply influenced by their shared Trinidadian background. Mama Fela herself was born and raised in Brooklyn... In this way, the school's adult population is explicitly global and the resultant culture within the building is a unique blend of traditions that is constantly evolving to encompass the range of local and international experiences within its walls.

While they identify with and take pride in the unique traits of their individual cultures, the women reflect regularly on their shared identities and motivations. "All of us identify in similar ways. We're all Black females, mostly raised working class... Everyone is here because they believe in the value of an African-centered curriculum." This affinity is a primary influence for how teaching is enacted. For instance, Mama Aaliyah grew up in the United States, surrounded by Black people who looked like her and shared the same cultural traditions. For her, "it's second nature to bring that into the classroom... if I'm picking a story to read, a story that reflects my [shared reality with the children] is going to be my first choice".

hooks (1994) named that "teachers must be actively committed to a process of self-actualization that promotes their own well-being if they are to teach in a manner that empowers students" (p. 15). Little Sun People is unique to many schools because it has figured out that when teachers are encouraged to explore their various identities and have the freedom and safety to bring their full selves into the workplace, they are both healthier and more fulfilled professionally. The result is an environment where children have strong models of self-expression early in life, both allowing them to see people that they are in community with living safely and authentically and giving them permission to practice living in their own authenticity at an early age (see Figure 10.1).

In practice, the work of this is a two-fold approach. When the women come to school wearing their natural hair with intention, can interact with

Self-Reflection

Figure 10.1 Teachers reflect on and model beauty by wearing clothes and prints from their countries of origin and encourage children to do the same as a way of counteracting messages that tell children that these places and ways of being are not valuable and as a way of connecting children to their community members in other parts of the world

colleagues without needing to code-switch, dress in ways that reflect the colors, patterns and styles of their home communities, etc., it is a direct challenge to messages in the world that have told both them and their children that who they are is not worthy of pride, beauty, authenticity and love of self. "Our children love it… we exude a pride in it… they say 'my teachers look good!' " Likewise, when Mama Aaliyah tells her children that they are intelligent and beautiful, just like the children in the book about children from West Africa, she is encouraging them to see themselves not only the way she sees them but the way she sees herself.

Teaching is work that requires ongoing self-examination of who the teachers are in the world and that self-examination directly impacts their dress, language, demeanor and interactions with their community. "It reminds me how much I love who I am." Witnessing this subversion of society's expectations of their beauty and self-identity, it becomes clear that the teachers themselves are practicing a form of global citizenship in a way that is restorative and healing. Regularly they are engaged in the act of appreciating their own identified heritage and community and, at the same time, are influenced by and absorb the benefits of the blended global community created when they come together to teach. Their children's success as confident, mentally and emotionally well members of their community is directly linked to the teachers' explorations and expressions of their identities and through this shared experience of being members of the diaspora.

The Work of Teachers

At Mid-Pacific, the preschool teachers spend a lot of time thinking about their identities as it relates to what brought them to teaching. Leslie often reflects on her upbringing in the Southern Appalachia and the development of her skills as an educator while working with very poor families. Jordan draws on her experience teaching art in a safe house for women and children early in her career and uses this experience to support the children and her colleagues in the use of materials to extend learning sensitively and creatively. Robynne, born and raised in Hawai'i, often reflects on the lessons she learned from a young age about respect for the elderly and a foundational mindset of gratitude, both of which consistently find their way into the curriculum. These divergent histories are valuable as educators coming together to support children from their own interesting variety of backgrounds. Learning to work together, and the pivots and adjustments necessary to do so successfully, has provided excellent practice for supporting children in doing a similar form of negotiation when they enter what is, for some, their first peer community.

For all of the ways that the teachers' histories may be dissimilar at Mid-Pacific, a clear alignment is in their shared belief in the value of the Reggio Emilia philosophy and its intention of positioning the child as a competent member of the community. Malaguzzi (2012, cited in Gandini, 2012) himself named that the goal of the work is to "reinforce each child's sense of identity through a recognition that comes from peers and adults, so much so that each one would feel enough sense of belonging and self-confidence to participate in the activities of the school" (p. 45). For children at Mid-Pacific, belonging and self-confidence come in the form of constant messaging, from the adults in their life, that their ideas are valuable and their differences are treasured enough to be reflected in the physical artifacts of the classroom, the wide and varied discussions that they so often lead, and the themes that are explored throughout the year.

For all the teachers, providing this space throughout the day for children's voices to be elevated is a response to intentional and sustained work understanding their own inclinations. If, for example, we were to return once more to the planning period for the children's visit to the capital for the memorial of the Queen's overthrow, we would find the teachers engaged in conversation about how much their own opinions could potentially influence the way the children understood the historic day. Without a pause for self-reflection, it would have been easy to create an experience that was not responsive to the child's learning needs in the moment.

148

Leslie is clear that "ultimately, it comes down to our image of who our children are. As teachers, we need to know our strengths and our weaknesses". The urge to insert one's personal beliefs is tempered by the importance of allowing children to make meaning and to build their ability to engage personally and independently with big and important ideas in the world. This skill is critically important in the life of the global citizen but can only be practiced early in life if the child has adults that are able to trust them enough to relinquish the urge to control the inquiry process. It is through the educators' self-reflective work that they are able to identify this urge within themselves. Only then are they able to adjust to craft experiences that honor their children's development, interest and abilities.

At both schools, the result of a self-reflective process is a more nuanced teaching style that acknowledges the child as a whole and complete person and children who are capable

> Where does self-reflection happen in your teaching practice?

of developing into confident and engaged community members. Families consistently report that children who graduate from Little Sun People show themselves to be self-aware and in control of both their voice and their narrative. According to one mother, commenting on her daughter's own self-identity development after being exposed to Little Sun People's community, "it was very matter of fact for her that being Black is cool". At Mid-Pacific, the teachers note that, each year, children learn to express agency and responsibility for their community. Like the class that decided that it would be them that would bring their concerns to the mayor's office, the practice of taking ownership for the betterment of their world is a natural result of their teachers' practice of trusting and respecting them.

It is important to note that, in both environments, it is not just the teachers doing this self-reflective work in a silo. Both teams are supported by administrators who have explicitly named this work as a priority for the betterment of their classrooms, school cultures and children's development as healthy and well-equipped community members. In addition to this articulation, both administrators have made choices that reflect their commitment to ensuring that reflective process is validated regularly in the lives of their teachers.

At Little Sun People, Mama Fela prioritizes an environment where teachers have endless opportunities to think about their cultural identities

The Work of Teachers

within the community. Not just children but teachers also see their heritages and teaching philosophies reflected in the curriculum. When negotiations with influencing local and state governing bodies occur, Mama Fela is resolute that the core theme of the teachers' (and the school's) reflective work, that the beauty and value of the children's community be infused into everything that they experience, not be compromised. This way, when teachers have identified their strengths and reflected on who they are as members of the diaspora, they have space to build these priorities into the day.

At Mid-Pacific, Dr. Hussey and the other administrators work regularly to cultivate an environment where teachers across the school feel that their working environment is one that recognizes the demanding (and sometimes divergent) priorities of being a teacher. The teaching team has expressed that even in exceptionally busy points of the year, time and space are regularly made to acknowledge the whole lives of the educators. Pausing to recognize important life events, incorporating teachers' passions (like Leslie's photography) and making room for moments to connect and reflect together, cultivates an environment where doing the work becomes more manageable and fulfilling which, in turn, leads to children's experiences in the classrooms that are more dynamic and joyful.

As educators, we bring pieces of ourselves to our teaching. Our identities. Our motivations. Our struggles and our challenges. It is unavoidable and makes us unique both individually and in teams. In this way we directly contribute to the atmosphere that children enter into and impact how they learn about themselves as members of a global community. In this demanding and, often, product-oriented profession, it is not always intuitive to pause and think about who we are and why we do what we do. At both Mid-Pacific and Little Sun People, teachers thrive in environments where space is intentionally made to do the work of reflecting on their identities. The result of this are environments where children are able to thrive as a result of both witnessing adults who are comfortable and safe being themselves and the pauses teachers take to make room for children's voices and ideas to shine.

Self-Reflection

Worksheet 10.1 Opportunities for Self-Reflection

Happens/Could Happen at Each Point in the Day					
Morning Prep?	Naptime/ Other Quiet Time?	Teacher Team Meetings?	Structured Professional Development?	After School Hours?	Other?

References

Gandini, L. (2012). History, ideas, and basic principles: An interview with Loris Malaguzzi. In C. Edwards, L. Gandini, & G. Forman (Eds.), *The hundred languages of children: The Reggio Emilia experience in transformation* (pp. 27–71). Praeger.

hooks, b. (1994). *Teaching to transgress: Education as the practice of freedom*. Routledge.

Collaboration

Collaborative work occurs at many different levels at both Mid-Pacific and Little Sun People. At Mid-Pacific, the documentation of the children's work, which teachers are constantly building through the year, creates a neutral connecting point for conversation. It can be a demanding process that often brings all hands on deck and requires a regular practice of negotiation of ideas and process. The team also prioritizes finding time throughout the week to connect (see Figure 11.1), not just on logistics and the running of the classroom but also about how to bring projects to life for the children.

With full days, collaboration sometimes happens in the moment and flexibility is required. Leslie will have an idea and it gets added to the morning meeting. While observing the interaction between children, Jordan may pull a teacher to the side and say, "I have an idea, what do you think?" Having a pedagogista in the classroom, whose primary role is to support the teachers in the development of their ideas and mull over questions together that arise among the children, is invaluable here. Robynne explains that having a school-wide culture that supports collaboration also contributes to an environment where it is natural for teachers to come together, within their own teams as well as with other teachers in other parts of the school, to talk and experience professional learning together.

Every Sunday, the teaching team at Little Sun People meets online to think together about the weeks and months ahead. It's both an informal and a structured space. Working from home, teachers are able to experience a level of comfort they might not access at school and discussions center on brainstorming, problem solving and mapping out the numerous priorities for the school space, depending on the time of year. For instance,

Figure 11.1 Collaboration and learning together as a teaching team at Mid-Pacific

in the spring of 2021, while this book was being written, the theme was baby humans, animals and plants, and all of the wondrous topics about growth and family and care that come with it. Together the team works to infuse the theme into the existing structure of the school and to tailor it to the children's interests.

> How has collaboration strengthened your community?

To navigate the abundance of skill at the school, the teaching team works to hear everyone's voice and play to each other's strengths. Mama Aaliyah shares that it takes time to learn where each teacher shines but once identified, the structure of the day comes together. She explains that "I try to let everyone do what's in their lane. One assistant really likes doing art projects. I'm very literacy based so I'm really into reading stories and having discussions with the kids. My other assistant is really into cooking and we do cooking on Fridays and she leads that". The day works best when everyone leans into their passion and teachers

Collaboration

find themselves more professionally fulfilled with the space and support to focus on work that satisfies them and brings them joy.

The mindset of gratitude and appreciation for one another that Robynne speaks of is particularly meaningful at Mid-Pacific. In conversation, the teachers exhibit a high level of respect for each other and it is something that they encourage among their children as well. That does not mean that they agree on everything. Ideas are tried out, the community is involved together and shared projects, like documentation, level the playing field. Similarly, the school-wide value of community creates an atmosphere where "you never feel isolated. You always feel you can go to the next room or building. We're here for each other, sharing ideas". The culture of care and belonging becomes a model for how the children interact with one another.

At Little Sun People, the relationship between the teachers, families and community creates an ecosystem for children where they are surrounded on all sides by examples of coexistence. Relationships are intentionally built year to year and each time an activity occurs, the message is reinforced. When a visitor is coming, teachers talk to the child about the visitor before and after and utilize materials and activities relevant to the role of that community member. For instance, when a drummer came to participate in the meeting between children at Little Sun People and another local school, their presence and music folded seamlessly into an ongoing unit that teachers regularly visit with the children that have them experiencing African drumming and dancing. Likewise, when the children visited the apple orchard (see Figure 11.2), the experiences was embedded in conversations about community, family, healthy eating and nature that had already been occurring between teachers and children.

With so much planning, thought processing and creation of documentation, time is at a premium at Mid-Pacific. Teachers are always looking for new and better ways to share with the community about what is happening in their class. "There's so much you want to do and endless amounts of documentation that we could do." There is also the pressure to stay on schedule with the various demands of the school year. Sometimes it feels like there's just not enough time. The teachers take it in their stride (see Figure 11.3). Robynne is candid about it being "mental work. Things come up. Sometimes you end up meeting on the go.". Sometimes opportunities come that the teachers stretch to take part in, despite the strain it adds to their already crowded schedule, because of the value it adds to

The Work of Teachers

Figure 11.2 Parents and teachers walk beside children exploring an apple orchard

Figure 11.3 A group of Mid-Pacific teachers head to a training on campus

Collaboration

their community. This is easier to do in an environment where the space expands and contracts regularly to acknowledge the needs of teachers. Feeling valued within a culture where flexibility already exists creates a receptive environment for tackling challenges together as a team.

Similarly, at Little Sun People, time is a luxury. The school day is long. The first students of the day arrive at or before 8:00 am and the last child who stays for after school goes home at 6:00 pm. The school has had to hire additional teachers to provide coverage because it is a demanding teaching day otherwise. "Children deserve engaged adults and we're doing it. We just get creative in finding time." The work of "finding time" is about thinking about the day differently. Teachers often eat breakfast and lunch together with children, which strengthens their bond. Family are "the heart of the school" and assist in all aspects of the community from cooking meals to volunteering service hours to serving on various committees, which frees up time for teachers to build and collaborate together.

A second level of collaboration at play in both schools is inter-school and inter-community collaboration. Both teaching teams spend time each year in conversation with other teachers and schools in environments different from their own. At times, these conversations are with communities which, though different, share common beliefs about teaching. At others, the teachers are interacting from across vastly different demographics *and* teaching philosophies.

Mama Fela has expressed the desire to partner with other schools for many years. As a graduate of Bank Street College of Education, she is in the habit of collaborating with school leaders from across the city, has seen the benefits of that collaboration in her own work, and desires a similar experience for her teachers and children. A new partnership with a school that is familiar in some ways and quite different from her own in others has been the result. Maple Street School is an early learning center located in the Prospect Lefferts Gardens neighborhood in Brooklyn. A cooperative (the families themselves own and operate the school), Maple Street espouses both Bank Street's Developmental Interaction Approach and the Reggio Emilia philosophy although by their own words "we believe that choosing one or even two philosophies is limiting for so many voices and needs" (www.maplestreetschool.org). The directors of the two schools initially served on a panel at Bank Street and formed a relationship through their shared alma mater. Although the demographics of the schools are different (Maple Street serves significantly more White, middle class

157

The Work of Teachers

families), "we decided that we'd love to be sister schools, share resources and have our children meet". Meetings began virtually with teachers and children sharing ideas for Black History Month and evolved to in-person gatherings. Art activities, curriculum shares and concerts in the park with parents, musicians and teachers from both schools has been the result.

The teachers at Mid-Pacific regularly collaborate with educators from other parts of the island as well. In addition to hosting workshops at their own campus, the group has visited with teachers on the windward side of the island (Oahu's east shore) and invited them to visit and observe their classroom in Mānoa Valley. At times the collaboration has challenged the teachers' ways of thinking about curriculum. During a visit to observe Mid-Pacific's classroom work, a group of educators questioned the team's use of fresh vegetables in manipulative play because it was food that could have been utilized in meals for people in need. The conversation caused the teachers to be both more intentional about their use of materials and more mindful about considering the impact of their teaching strategies and their vision for their children's learning experiences on the very real needs of others in their community.

> What are the biggest challenges to establishing a culture of collaboration within your school? With other schools?

In their collaborative work with various Kumu from the Hawaiian community, the teachers are also regularly adjusting their understanding and beliefs. The team works to center the expertise and knowledge of these teachers, cultivating relationships that Trask (1999) identified as being rooted in implicit trust. Part of this work is an acknowledgement, on the Mid-Pacific team's part, that their role is not to tell others who hold indigenous knowledges what to do and how to practice but to support them in the perpetuation of said practice. Good allyship then becomes a necessary aspect of effective collaboration.

Motivated, in a similar way as Little Sun People, by the benefit of engaging in intellectual conversations with others as a way of strengthening each other's practice, the experience of collaborating with schools from other international communities has benefited the team in profound ways as well. In the case of the South Africa partnership, teachers found commonality as the school in South Africa also exists within the context of a culture that places great importance on both the children's connection to the community and to the land around them. For the Mid-Pacific team, it has been validating to encounter a school in a different part of the world with similar values and to expose their children to another corner of their community through this partnership.

Engaging in any level of collaborative work is risky. It is especially vulnerable work to share and engage in ways that shift and build the culture of a school in favor of children's experiences as members of the community. However, as Robynne says, the risk-taking creates "opportunities to learn from each other" as well as to benefit children through the teaching team's shared vision. hooks (1994) expands on this in her explanation of the engaged voice as one that must resist being fixed but instead should reflect on the work as always changing, updating and being in relationship with the needs of the world around it. At both Mid-Pacific and Little Sun People, teachers engage in this type of responsive work as their needs and the needs of their children reveal themselves. It is necessary work not only because it exhibits a flexibility in an ever-changing world but also, and perhaps more importantly, because it models for children the kind of collaboration necessary to live successfully in a world full of diverse perspectives with respect for each voice.

Conclusion

Self-reflection and collaboration is a two-part strategy that has been shown to be effective at both Little Sun People and Mid-Pacific preschool in supporting the teacher practice of delivering effective global citizenship education to their students. Although the two schools sometimes utilize different strategies and serve different demographics, the ways that teachers interrogate and then integrate their own perspectives as well as collaborate with one another and with their extended community is a necessary resource for the healthy life of their schools. In witnessing their process, children have a mirror with which to practice identifying their own voices and successfully using them in the surrounding world to build a healthy and affirming community for one another.

The Work of Teachers

Worksheet 11.1 Strengthening Our Collaborative Practice

Consider your goal.

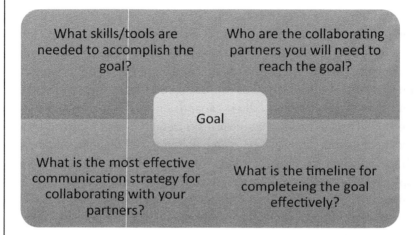

Reflection

What worked? What needs adjusting?

What additional steps might be necessary to accommodate your goal? Your community's needs?

What are the ways that this practice can strengthen your neighborhood? Your school? Your local community? Your global community?

References

hooks, b. (1994). *Teaching to transgress: Education as the practice of freedom*. Routledge.

Maple Street School. www.maplestreetschool.org

Trask, H. (1999). *From a native daughter: Colonialism and sovereignty in Hawai'i*. University of Hawai'i Press.

Afterword

When asked what their hopes are for their children, the teachers from both Little Sun People and Mid-Pacific Institute share that they desire for their children to have an awareness of their value and of their responsibilities as members of extraordinary communities.

> "My hope for them is that they are respectful, kind, good people who find happiness in sharing their gifts with others."
>
> "That they never lose the joy of this journey no matter where they are. The joy for learning. The joy for wondering."
>
> "Just for them to be all that they can be and to remember themselves. To remember the greatness of their people."
>
> "My hope is that they remember community."

Community. Remembering. Wondering. The sharing of gifts. Respect. Joy. Childs (1998) asks how can we facilitate the coming together of many different kinds of people to build a world where freedom and justice exist for everyone? The teachers at these two schools have no trouble naming the elements required to do this work. I am reminded, again, of the Capitol insurrection and the fear and anger on the faces of thousands of people as they broke down doors and hunted for politicians whose beliefs they did not agree with. I cannot help but wonder who those people might have been had they been given the opportunity to practice the elements of global citizenship in this text in their earliest years. Global education's dove-tailed work of being both an anti-colonial approach that disrupts oppressive narratives by elevating the local community and what Childs calls the Transcommunal Approach, which welcomes many different perspectives with respect and mutual recognition, has the power to guide today's child towards another way.

Much like Genishi and Goodwin's (2008) refusal, in their study of diversity in early childhood education, to conclude that there is only one definition of social justice, I resist a single definition of global citizenship education. The two preschools presented in this text could not be more different. The purposeful pairing of the two here was created with a couple of goals in mind. It is hoped that this text would contribute to the body of resources available to early educators, scholars and community members in search of strategies for supporting young children's development as global citizens. It is also hoped that this text would spark conversation between early educators and global educators to think more expansively about what effective global citizenship education can look like across a variety of spaces that support young children's learning.

In my work, I encourage teachers with questions about how to build more global learning into their day to spend time observing and listening to their children. It is likely that there is much documented here that is already occurring in your classroom or in your life with young children. Listening to and making space for children's voices and their questions about their world will always be the best first step. From there, the work is not about adding an occasional experience to a pre-existing curriculum but about fully integrating what children bring (their perspectives, their questions and wonderings, their families, cultures and communities) into the daily life of our programs. It is in this type of environment that children learn early that their identities and ways of knowing are meant to be seen and valued and that others do not serve simply as a supplement to their existence but as full-fledged community members alongside them.

References

Childs, J. B. (1998). Transcommunality: From the politics of conversion to the ethics of respect in the context of cultural diversity – learning from native American philosophies with a focus on the Haudenosaunee. *Social Justice*, 25(4), 143–169.

Genishi, C., & Goodwin, A. (Eds.) (2008). *Diversities in early childhood education: Rethinking and doing*. Routledge.

Appendices

Appendix A. Useful Websites and Online Resources

www.bankstreet.edu/about-bank-street/our-approach

https://childcare.gov/consumer-education/family-child-care-homes

www.circleofsecurityinternational.com

http://delawaretribe.org

https://earlylearning.hawaii.gov

www.hawaiipublicschools.org

www.littlesunpeople.com

https://native-land.ca

www.maplestreetschool.org

www.midpac.edu/about

https://pacthawaii.org

https://reggioalliance.org

https://restorationplaza.org

www.thirteen.org/brooklyn/history/history2.html

Appendix B. Commonly Used Terms, Phrases and Locations

'Aina: land/people/country

Ali'i: Chief

Baba: term of respect used to refer to an older man at Little Sun People

Bedford-Stuyvesant/Bed-Stuy: Neighborhood in Northern Central Brooklyn which has undergone significant cultural shifts and is the current home of Little Sun People, Inc.

Elemakule: the elderly

Kapu: moral code

Kumu: teacher

Kupuna: grandparent

Lei: flower garland to welcome a visitor, to celebrate a special occasion, e.g. birthday, wedding, graduation, etc. Each flower represents individuals connected as a community

Mama: term of respect used to refer to an older woman at Little Sun People

Mana: spiritual power

Mānoa Valley: region of the island of Oahu situated three miles east of Honolulu where Mid-Pacific Institute is located.

Maunakea: a mountain and sacred site on the island of Hawai'i

'Ohana: extended family

'Okana: district or region

Restoration Plaza/Restoration: former site of the Sheffield Farms Milk Bottling Plant and current home to a primary arts and business hub in Bedford-Stuyvesant

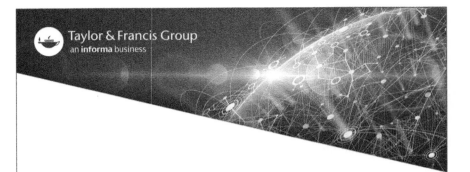